PICKFORD

MATT AND TOM OLDFIELD

ULTIMATE
FOOTBALL HEROES

PICKFORD

FROM THE PLAYGROUND
TO THE PITCH

DINO

Published by Dino Books,
an imprint of John Blake Publishing,
2.25, The Plaza,
535 Kings Road,
Chelsea Harbour,
London SW10 0SZ

www.johnblakepublishing.co.uk

www.facebook.com/johnblakebooks 🆕
twitter.com/jblakebooks 🆕

This edition published in 2018

ISBN: 978 1 78946 052 0

British Library Cataloguing-in-Publication Data:

A catalogue record for this book is available from the British Library.

Design by www.envydesign.co.uk

Printed and bound in Great Britain by Clays Ltd, Elcograf S.p.A.

1 3 5 7 9 10 8 6 4 2

Papers used by John Blake Publishing are natural, recyclable products made from wood
grown in sustainable forests. The manufacturing processes conform to the environmental
regulations of the country of origin.

Every reasonable effort has been made to trace copyright-holders of material reproduced in
this book, but if any have been inadvertently overlooked the publishers would be glad to
hear from them.

John Blake Publishing is an imprint of Bonnier Books UK
www.bonnierbooks.co.uk

For all readers,
young and old(er)

ULTIMATE
FOOTBALL HEROES

Matt Oldfield is an accomplished writer and the editor-in-chief
of football review site *Of Pitch & Page*. Tom Oldfield is a freelance
sports writer and the author of biographies on Cristiano Ronaldo,
Arsène Wenger and Rafael Nadal.

Cover illustration by Dan Leydon.
To learn more about Dan visit danleydon.com
To purchase his artwork visit etsy.com/shop/footynews
Or just follow him on Twitter @danleydon

TABLE OF CONTENTS

ACKNOWLEDGEMENTS 9

CHAPTER 1 – ENGLAND'S PENALTY HERO 11

CHAPTER 2 – SAFE HANDS 22

CHAPTER 3 – CATCHING SUNDERLAND'S EYE 28

CHAPTER 4 – SCHOOL TEAM STRIKER 34

CHAPTER 5 – MOVIES WITH MEGAN 42

CHAPTER 6 – CONFIDENT CHARACTER 48

CHAPTER 7 – WORLD CUP WOBBLE 54

CHAPTER 8 – THE DEEP END AT DARLINGTON 59

CHAPTER 9 – LEARNING TO LOSE 70

CHAPTER 10 – AMAZING AT ALFRETON 75

CHAPTER 11 – **ON THE MOVE AGAIN** 81

CHAPTER 12 – **BRAVERY AT BRADFORD**. 87

CHAPTER 13 – **IMPRESSING AT PRESTON** 93

CHAPTER 14 – **FINALLY!** 98

CHAPTER 15 – **SUNDERLAND'S NUMBER 1** 105

CHAPTER 16 – **EVERTON AND THE EUROS** 117

CHAPTER 17 – **EVERTON DAYS** 123

CHAPTER 18 – **WEMBLEY WONDER**. 128

CHAPTER 19 – **WORLD CUP ADVENTURE BEGINS** 134

CHAPTER 20 – **SHOOT-OUT STAR**. 144

CHAPTER 21 – **RETURNING AS HEROES** 149

ACKNOWLEDGEMENTS

First of all, I'd like to thank John Blake Publishing –
and particularly my editor James Hodgkinson – for
giving me the opportunity to work on these books
and for supporting me throughout. Writing stories for
the next generation of football fans is both an honour
and a pleasure.

I wouldn't be doing this if it wasn't for my brother
Tom. I owe him so much and I'm very grateful for
his belief in me as an author. I feel like Robin setting
out on a solo career after a great partnership with
Batman. I hope I do him (Tom, not Batman) justice
with these new books.

Next up, I want to thank my friends for keeping

me sane during long hours in front of the laptop.
Pang, Will, Mills, Doug, John, Charlie – the laughs
and the cups of coffee are always appreciated.

I've already thanked my brother but I'm also very
grateful to the rest of my family, especially Melissa,
Noah and of course Mum and Dad. To my parents, I
owe my biggest passions: football and books. They're
a real inspiration for everything I do.

Finally, I couldn't have done this without Iona's
encouragement and understanding during long,
work-filled weekends. Much love to you.

CHAPTER 1

ENGLAND'S PENALTY HERO

Otkritie Arena, Moscow, 3 July 2018

The tired England team assembled on the pitch. After 120 nail-biting minutes, only a penalty shoot-out stood between them and the World Cup quarter-finals. They needed a hero. Could it be their young keeper, playing in only his seventh international match? Jordan took a deep breath and believed.

Colombia's late equaliser had been a crushing blow. After making a super save to deny Mateus Uribe, Jordan just couldn't keep out Yerry Mina's powerful header.

'Now we'll just have to do it the hard way,' Jordan said to himself.

Still, Gareth Southgate looked like the calmest person in the stadium. 'Okay lads, we knew penalties were part of the deal in the knockout rounds,' he said. 'We're ready for this.'

Jordan nodded. They had spent hours practising on the training ground to make sure that they were all as comfortable as possible if it came to this.

He watched Gareth walk from player to player, checking on injuries and last-minute confidence levels.

'All good?' he asked Marcus and Kieran.

Both looked straight at their manager and nodded. No hesitation. While the physios worked quickly to heal players' tired legs, Gareth wrote down five names on a sheet of paper for the referee:

Harry Kane, Marcus Rashford, Jordan Henderson (or Hendo, as everyone called him), Kieran Trippier, Eric Dier.

'Remember everything we've talked about,' Harry shouted over the noise from the crowd. 'Pick your spot and be decisive. Don't feel rushed, and just ignore their keeper.'

'Come on, boys!' Jordan yelled, jumping up and down to release some of the nervous energy.

Jordan had his own plan to follow. After watching hundreds of clips of penalties on his laptop, he had sat down with England's other goalkeepers, Jack Butland and Nick Pope, to decide on the team tactics. Which way should he dive for each of Colombia's takers? He was leaving nothing to chance.

'Here you go,' Jack said, handing him a water bottle, which had notes written on it. 'Good luck!'

'Thanks, mate!' Jordan replied.

He gripped the bottle tightly as he read the words. He felt ready for the biggest moment of his life.

Harry was back from the coin toss. 'We're going second, lads,' he said.

Gareth had a few final words: 'I'm so proud of all of you. So are all the fans. This is just one more test laid out in front of us. Now go and be heroes!' The players all clapped and cheered.

As they walked over to the halfway line, Gareth put his arm around Jordan. 'There isn't any other shot-stopper in the world I'd want protecting our net tonight. Just trust your instincts.'

Jordan felt ten feet tall. He didn't know what to say so he just high-fived Gareth and then jogged over to the far end of the pitch. He was in his zone now, but he took a minute to glance at the England flags behind the goal. Even from a distance, he could see the passion. There was fear too. Penalties had not been kind to England in the past. In fact, they had never won a World Cup shoot-out. Ever!

'You can do this, Jordan!' the supporters shouted. He winked back at them. Yes, he could!

As he walked over to the goal, Jordan tucked his bottle into a red towel so that the Colombia keeper wouldn't spot England's secret plan. What if David Ospina asked to have a sip of water? That would be a disaster!

Luckily, he didn't. Jordan took one last look at his bottle and then stepped onto his line. Radamel Falcao was up first. Jordan waited as long as he could before diving to his right, but Falcao placed it perfectly down the middle. 1–0!

Jordan dragged himself up, shaking his head. 'Forget it and move on,' he told himself. There would be other chances to save the day.

He had a more important job to do first. He grabbed the ball and carried it over to Harry. This was part of Gareth's plan. It gave the Colombian keeper one fewer reason to approach the England penalty takers to put them off.

'You've got this, big man,' he said, patting Harry on the shoulder.

Harry smashed his penalty into the bottom corner. Unstoppable – 1–1!

Jordan guessed the right way on Colombia's second penalty, but Juan Cuadrado picked out the top corner. 2–1!

When Marcus' perfect strike made it 2–2, the pressure went up another level. On his way back to the halfway line, Marcus ran over to Jordan to bump fists. 'We believe in you, man,' he said, pointing at his goalkeeper as he walked away. 'A big save is coming. I know it!'

Colombia made no mistake with their third

penalty either. Jordan tried not to panic. He was getting a good spring off his line, but the Colombians had not given him a sniff so far. Still, he could see that they had put all their best penalty takers first.

Seconds later, his heart sank. Hendo hit his penalty well but the Colombian keeper guessed right and pushed it out... *Saved!*

Now Jordan really had to step up, or England's World Cup dream would be over.

He went through the same routine again: bouncing on his line, making himself big, timing his dive. He correctly guessed left for the fourth penalty but saw the ball fly high above his dive. He turned to see it crash off the bar and bounce safely away from the goal... *Miss!*

'Yeeeeeeees!' he screamed, looking over at his teammates. The England fans roared. They were back in it.

Kieran kept his nerve with a beautiful penalty. 3–3! It was basically sudden death now.

Jordan tried to stay calm but his heart was racing after the Colombia miss. He felt even more confident now.

'One stop, one stop,' he mumbled under his breath. That might be all it took to become England's penalty hero.

As Carlos Bacca stepped up for Colombia's fifth penalty, the crowd fell silent. Jordan watched Bacca run up and then he sprung to his right. His eyes lit up as the ball curled towards him. But he was diving too far. Almost in slow motion, he threw up his left hand desperately. The ball was well hit but his hand stayed strong, clawing the penalty away... *Saved!*

'Come ooooooooooooooon!'

Jordan leapt to his feet and punched the air again and again, screaming as loud as he could. The plan had worked. He had just saved a penalty in a World Cup shoot-out! Now England were one kick away from the quarter-finals.

He looked towards the halfway line and saw the huge smiles on his teammates' faces. They stood with their arms linked, ready to sprint forward if everything went to plan.

Jordan felt like he was shaking as he passed the

ball to Eric, but he tried not to show it. 'Just take your time,' he said.

Eric did just that. He paced out his run-up, waited for the whistle and then swept the ball low into the bottom corner. England had done it!

The next few minutes were a blur. Jordan leapt in the air and turned to run towards the halfway line. But he was too late. His teammates were already racing over to *him*, England's penalty hero. Harry and Kieran jumped on his back. Then John Stones and Marcus, followed by the whole team.

'You legend!' Kieran screamed.

'I owe you big time!' Hendo called, ruffling Jordan's hair.

Jordan savoured every second with his teammates, who had become his friends over the past few weeks. They hugged and laughed as it all began to sink in. Happiness, relief and exhaustion – all the emotions mixed together.

Gareth joined in the celebrations, hugging every player and saving the biggest one for Jordan. 'I told you!' he laughed, jabbing Jordan playfully in the ribs. 'I knew you'd do something special tonight.'

Then they ran over to the fans – or limped over, in most cases. Tomorrow, they would be sore, but tonight they were buzzing too much to feel it. The England players had given their nation something to really cheer about.

'They've had to wait a long time for this!' Jordan shouted to Harry.

'Get right at the front, Jordan. You're the hero tonight!' Harry nudged him forward, so that the fans could sing his name:

Rhythm is a dancer,
Pickford is the answer,
Saving shots from everywhere!

Jordan couldn't believe what he was hearing. What a feeling! The players took photo after photo before finally reaching the section where their families stood waiting. He spotted his girlfriend, Megan, in the crowd and blew her a kiss. It meant so much that she was in the stadium to see it all. He could only imagine the celebrations back in England. He remembered that a lot of his friends had been planning to watch the game together, and that made him even prouder.

Jordan could feel happy tears building up and the hairs on the back of his neck stood on end. He just didn't want the night to end. The England fans were in no hurry to go home either.

When the players finally got back to the dressing room, Gareth called for quiet.

'Lads, take a moment to think about what you've just achieved. I could not be prouder of every single one of you. That took guts. We had to fight for everything. They kicked us all over the pitch, but we kept our cool and never gave up.

'And those were terrific penalties, including yours Hendo. I will remember this moment for a very long time. Let's enjoy it tonight. You deserve that. But we've got more memories to make, starting with either Sweden or Switzerland on Saturday. This is just the beginning for this team!'

The players did not have the energy to stand up,

but they clapped and cheered. Jordan was so happy for his manager, who had famously dealt with penalty shoot-out heartbreak as an England player, back at Euro 96.

There was only one song for the players to sing. Eric turned on the music and cranked up the volume:

'It's coming home, it's coming home,
It's coming, FOOTBALL'S COMING HOME!'

'If you'd told me five years ago that I'd be saving a penalty at the 2018 World Cup, I'd have laughed in your face,' Jordan told Kieran, giggling. 'I was playing in League Two! It's been such a crazy journey, but it's all worth it now. It doesn't get any better than this!'

As he took off his socks and grabbed a towel, Jordan thought about his journey again – the highs, the lows, the doubts. He was still only twenty-four, but it had been quite a ride so far!

CHAPTER 2

SAFE HANDS

Jordan's love of football had been there from the beginning, but his sixth birthday gave him an extra push.

After a fun party with his friends, it was time to open his presents. His parents' first job was to get him to sit still. He had grabbed a second helping of cake and ice cream, and he was now busy running from room to room.

'Okay, Jordan,' his mum called. 'We'll give these presents back if you don't want to open them.'

'What? No, Mam! I'm coming,' Jordan shouted. He zoomed into the room and sat on the sofa, breathing heavily.

He opened each present in a hurry, tearing the wrapping paper excitedly. Before long, there was a pile of unwrapped gifts on one of the chairs: a painting set, a wooly jumper and an animal book, and a Sunderland Football Club T-shirt. Jordan's parents were both Newcastle United fans but despite their best efforts, Jordan had decided to support their rivals in red and white.

'Okay, open this one next,' his dad said, passing a present to Jordan and then picking up the camera.

Jordan tried to feel through the paper and guess what it might be, but he had no idea. He unwrapped it and found a pair of red and white goalkeeper gloves. 'Wow, these are so cool – thanks!'

His dad grinned. 'We've heard you talking about being a keeper. Now you can give it a try!'

Jordan's brother, Richard, was delighted too. Now he would have someone to test his shooting against.

Jordan turned to his friends. 'Come on. Let's go outside and test them out.' He found his brother in the kitchen. 'Richard, bring your ball!'

His mum started to remind the boys that it would

be cold outside and then stopped herself. That was hardly going to stop them!

Seconds later, they heard the ball bouncing around outside. 'At least they'll sleep well tonight,' Jordan's dad said with a grin as they finished clearing up.

For the next few weeks, Jordan's parents got used to hearing their sons playing outside every night until dinner time. They had marked out a goal on the fence and Jordan always had to be the keeper. Richard was six years older than Jordan and he could kick the ball really powerfully. BANG!

At first, Jordan had no chance but, with practice, he got better and better. He was desperate to beat his elder brother. He loved flinging himself across the goal and stretching his arms out wide to try and block the shots. The only problem? It was mostly concrete outside, but that didn't stop Jordan from diving for everything.

'Alright, let's take a look at the damage today,' his mum said as they sat down for dinner one night. It had become a regular task to check Jordan's knees and elbows and clean up any cuts. 'Why don't you just take the ball to the park instead? It's a good job we buy the family size box of plasters these days!'

'Ouch,' Jordan said. 'That scab is the worst one. I keep cutting it open.'

'I wonder why,' his mum replied, smiling and shaking her head.

A week later, Jordan made three diving saves in a row, drawing more blood under his shirt. 'Hey, you're getting really good, lad!' Richard called out as he chased after the ball. 'I don't want you to get too cocky, but you should think about joining a team.'

Jordan grinned and grinned. How cool would that be? That night, he stared at the ceiling and imagined himself saving shot after shot for Sunderland. One minute it was a daring dive to tip a high shot over the bar, the next it was a low shot that he tipped around the post.

'Yet another super save from Pickford!' the TV commentator would say.

The more he played in goal with his brother, the more Jordan could picture becoming a professional goalkeeper one day. Plus, he would be an even better

keeper when he was diving on grass instead
of concrete!

To prepare himself, Jordan watched his hero
Thomas Sørensen, Sunderland's Number 1.
Whenever he was playing on TV, he would pay
special attention to Sørensen's positioning and how
quickly and cleverly he released the ball to his
teammates.

'What a throw that was!' he cheered as The Black
Cats broke away on the counter-attack.

Jordan knew that goalkeepers had to be brave, have
good reactions and come flying out for crosses. He
knew that he could do all of those things, and more.

A few days later, while helping to clear plates from
the table, Jordan asked his dad a question that had
been on his mind a lot lately.

'Dad, could I start playing for a team at the
weekends? I really want to see if I'm any good in a
proper game.'

'Of course, Jordan,' his dad replied. 'Leave it with
me and I'll see what I can find out. There are lots of
local leagues around here.'

'Okay, thanks!' Jordan said, skipping towards the stairs.

'Good goalkeepers are hard to find!' his dad called over his shoulder.

That turned out to be true. One weekend, Jordan was watching his brother play when someone called out from a pitch nearby: 'Anyone want to play in goal? We need a keeper!'

'Me, I'll do it!' Jordan shouted out straight away.

'Great, have you got any gloves?'

'Yes, right here!'

Jordan had been carrying them around for weeks, waiting for his big chance to use them. Finally, it had arrived. He was so excited to test himself in a real league and do his best Sørensen impression.

CHAPTER 3

CATCHING SUNDERLAND'S EYE

Jordan was too busy playing football to notice, but his talent had been spotted. During an end of season tournament, he had led his team all the way to the semi-finals. Strikers fired in shot after shot but he was unbeatable at times. His dad told him that in one of their 1–0 wins, he counted ten saves.

'That might be a new record!' Jordan declared proudly.

But losing was painful. He was almost in tears about not reaching the final. He said goodbye to his teammates and headed to the car to wait for his dad. What was taking him so long?

There were a lot of pitches side-by-side and it

took Jordan a few minutes to work out where his dad was. From a distance, he saw him talking to a tall man in a tracksuit. He rolled his eyes, thinking his dad was probably in the middle of some kind of football debate.

When his dad finally got back to the car, he had a big grin on his face.

'Who was that?' Jordan asked. 'One of your friends?'

'Not exactly, no. Something a bit more exciting than that.'

Jordan was too tired and too disappointed to ask more questions.

His dad turned to look at him. 'That's it? You've usually got a hundred questions on this kind of thing!'

'Okay, you win. Who was it?'

'His name is Wayne Walls and he's a scout at Sunderland.'

That caught Jordan's attention. 'What?! What was he talking to you about?'

'He just wanted to know what time it was and whether there was a train station near here.'

'Oh.'

'I'm joking, Jordan. He was asking about *you*! He wants you to come for some training sessions at the Sunderland academy.'

Jordan punched the air and nearly jumped out of his seat. 'That's amazing! I had no idea there would be scouts at this tournament.'

'Trust me, I was surprised too! They want us to go up there on Wednesday night to fill out some forms, and then your first training session is on Thursday.'

Suddenly losing in the tournament didn't feel so bad. 'Wow, I can't wait to tell all my mates! They won't believe it.'

Jordan got a quick look around the facilities when he went to sign the forms, but it was nothing compared to the full tour on the Thursday night. He saw where the professionals changed, had lunch and did their gym work-outs. After that, Wayne met Jordan to show him the youth team changing room and hand over a pile of kit, all with the Sunderland badge on it.

'Thanks!' Jordan said, trying hard not to smile too much.

He put on the kit and stood in front of the mirror – just to make sure that it was all real. Yes, his dream really was coming true!

Soon, other boys arrived, and Wayne gave a big introduction: 'Everyone, this is Jordan, our new goalkeeper!'

With all the excitement, he had forgotten about being nervous. But now, the pressure was on. As Jordan walked out with all the other boys, who had all been there much longer, he worried that he might embarrass himself. What if they were way better than the players he had faced so far? What if they scored against him every time? Would he be invited back again?

He pushed all those thoughts to the side and reminded himself that he was there for a reason. Wayne had seen something at that tournament and now Jordan had to prove that he was right.

Before they played any kind of five-a-side game, there were various drills. For some of those drills,

Jordan was in goal, but for others he was expected to do the same things as the outfield players. He quickly saw that he was more comfortable than the two other goalkeepers with the ball at his feet. He probably had Richard to thank for that because they had been practising passing a lot lately.

When it came to the crossing and shooting exercises, Jordan barely made a mistake. He came out confidently to grab the ball, whether it was swinging in or away. He could tell that the strikers were better than the boys he usually faced, but he made save after save. He even made a double save from a striker called Barney. Jordan pushed away the first shot then jumped up to tip the second one round the post.

'Oh come on,' Barney yelled in frustration. 'Do you ever let a goal in?'

Jordan smiled. He already felt like he belonged.

Barney's next shot slipped through his hands and into the bottom corner. He slapped the ground. 'You got me that time,' Jordan said. He knew he should have saved it, but he never let those things get him down. He was already thinking about the next shot and his next save.

At the end of the session, Jordan walked over to see his dad, and Wayne joined them.

'Terrific start tonight,' he said, tapping Jordan on the head. 'Those strikers will be having nightmares about facing you!'

'I've got to make sure they're sharp enough for the real games,' Jordan replied with a smile.

'Well, I'll leave you to join the others and get changed. I just wanted to say well done.'

Once Wayne had gone, Jordan's dad came over and gave him a big hug. 'I'm so glad I was here to watch you tonight. Just know that I'm very proud.'

'Not in front of everyone, Dad!' Jordan groaned with embarrassment, before jogging back towards the changing rooms to join his new Sunderland teammates.

CHAPTER 4

SCHOOL TEAM STRIKER

Jordan was certain that he wanted to be a goalkeeper. He loved the pressure and the chance to be the hero. As he settled in at Sir Robert of Newminster Catholic School, he found that he was a natural at other sports too, including tennis and cross country running. But football was always his first love and, even though he was training with Sunderland, he had found a way to play with his friends on the school team too.

One morning, he rushed over to Mr Welch, who ran the school team.

'Mr Welch!' he called. 'Great news! Sunderland said it was ok for me to play for the school. So, what you do think? I can bring my gloves to training tomorrow.'

Mr Welch grinned. Jordan had been talking about this for weeks. 'That's great news, Jordan. We've got a good group this year and they'll all be doing backflips when they hear you're joining us. But don't bother bringing your gloves.'

Jordan was confused. 'Why not? I don't understand.'

'Well, I was thinking that you probably spend lots of time in goal for Sunderland with all those training sessions and youth team matches. I've seen you playing outfield in the playground. How would you like to play up front for us?'

Jordan laughed, thinking it was a joke, but one look at Mr Welch's face showed that it wasn't. 'You're serious? Oh wow, okay. Yeah, that sounds amazing. I've got a good strike on me.'

He stepped back and pretended to fire a shot into the top corner.

'Alright then. So, my challenge to you is to score ten goals this season.'

'Challenge accepted!'

In his first training session, a few of his friends cheered loudly as he jogged onto the pitch.

'Please welcome Sunderland's future number one keeper, Jordan Pickford!' Connor called out, doing his best stadium announcer voice.

'Fans, you can queue up for autographs over on the left,' added Dave, giggling. 'Don't worry, he's got time for all of you.'

Jordan laughed loudly. 'Good one!'

'We're just teasing,' Connor replied. 'Now that you're going to be playing for us, we can beat anyone.'

Jordan was excited to practise with his friends, but he hadn't played as a striker in a proper game. What if he was rubbish?

When they started a six-a-side game, his first pass went straight out for a throw-in.

'Better put him back in goal, Mr Welch!' shouted Dave. Jordan felt his cheeks go red, but he turned to Dave and gave him an 'I'm-watching-you' gesture.

Jordan quickly got comfortable. He scored three

goals and was easily the fastest player on the pitch.

'Hey, I thought you were a goalie!' joked Alfie, one of the team's defenders, after one long range strike. 'Goalies aren't supposed to be able to do that!'

Jordan smiled. 'I'm not your average keeper!'

As he helped collect the cones and balls, Jordan quizzed Mr Welch about the team's first game.

'It'll be here next Wednesday afternoon,' Mr Welch explained. 'The team will go up on the noticeboard on Tuesday morning.'

Jordan had faced plenty of nervy situations waiting for news about his place at Sunderland but, for some reason, he was just as worried about making the school team.

'If I'm on the bench, it'll be pretty embarrassing,' he told his mum on Monday night. 'They all know that I'm training at Sunderland!'

His mum's advice – to just relax and wait – proved to be right. When the teamsheet went up, Jordan saw his name near the bottom of the list. That told him he was probably starting up front.

When the bell sounded at the end of Wednesday

morning classes, Jordan raced to his locker and grabbed his bag. He spotted Connor and Alfie walking down the corridor towards him.

'It's game day!' shouted Alfie, scaring a handful of boys and girls standing near the water fountain.

As Jordan put on his kit, he could feel the excitement in the changing room. Even though the boys had just started at their new school, they were all desperate to do well.

'Did you know the results go up on the board?' Dave said. 'We've got to get off to a good start.'

From the first whistle, Jordan was everywhere, desperately chasing after every chance to score. He had to bend over and catch his breath a few times, but he hardly stopped running.

'Alfie, any chance you get, send the ball over the top!' he called, signalling where he wanted it.

A few minutes later, Alfie hooked the ball clear but it turned into the perfect pass. Jordan got to the ball before the defender and knocked it ahead. Now it was a straight sprint and there was only going to be one winner. As Jordan raced clear, he started thinking about his shot. He couldn't just blast the ball like a goal kick. Instead, he took his time and poked it into the bottom corner.

Goooooooooooooooooooooaaaaaaaaaaaaaaaaaalllllllllllll llllllllllllllll!!!!!!!!!!!!!!!!!!!

He ran over towards the corner flag, and then stopped. What should he do? He had never really needed a goal celebration before. He was a goalkeeper, after all! In the end, he just waited for his teammates to rush over and high-five him.

Connor put his arm round his shoulder. 'You're like lightning, Picky! Their defenders have no chance.'

'Just keep knocking it through. If they start putting two defenders on me, just take the ball yourself from midfield.'

'We're calling you Speedy from now on!' joked Mr Welch at half-time, pointing at Jordan. 'That was a great run.'

'Well how about Speedy scores another one, so we can relax back here!' Alfie replied.

'Deal!' Jordan said.

In the second half, he had two, sometimes three,

defenders following him around the pitch. There was always one dropping further back so that he couldn't just outrun them.

When the ball went out for a goal kick, Jordan ran over to Connor and whispered in his ear. 'Look for the quick one-two.'

The next time Jordan got the ball, he saw the defenders run backwards, expecting him to turn and run past them. Instead, he spun the other way and dribbled across the pitch towards Connor. Just as one defender lunged at the ball, Jordan fired it to Connor and then kept running. Connor took a touch, looked up to see where Jordan would be, and flicked the ball into a gap. One-two!

Jordan was on it in a flash, but he knew he only had a second to take his shot. He moved the ball onto his stronger left foot and hit the hardest shot he could. BANG! Just like this brother had taught him.

He was barged to the floor a second later but rolled over in time to see the ball in the back of the net and a disappointed goalkeeper with his hands on his head.

Goooooooooooooooooooooaaaaaaaaaaaaaaaaaalllllllllllll llllllllllllll!!!!!!!!!!!!!!!!!!!!

Before he could get up, Connor jumped on him. 'What a shot!' he yelled.

It felt great to get the first win of the year, and Jordan got pats on the backs from every player as they walked off the pitch.

'That was some debut!' Mr Welch said, appearing next to him. 'Make sure you thank your coaches at Sunderland for us.' They both laughed.

'Only eight more goals to go,' Jordan replied. 'We didn't agree on a prize, did we? Maybe I could have a few nights with no homework?'

'No chance!' Mr Welch said, shaking his head and grinning.

As Jordan walked home that night, he couldn't stop smiling, even though his legs were aching.

'I guess I'll have to get used to all this running,' he said out loud to himself.

As Sunderland's keeper and his school's striker, Jordan had a really fun season ahead of him.

CHAPTER 5

MOVIES WITH MEGAN

Most of Jordan's time was divided between
Sunderland and the school team. If he wasn't playing
football, he was usually thinking about it. But
recently, there had been a third thing on his mind:
Megan Davison.

'Want to come over and watch the Sunderland
game tomorrow night?' Connor asked one morning
on the way to their first lesson of the day.

'Sure,' Jordan replied. 'I just hope they play better
than they did last week.'

'Do you think they'll make some changes up
front?' Connor replied. 'We need to do something to
freshen things up and…'

He paused and looked at Jordan, who was staring across the corridor.

'Why don't you just go and say hi to her?' Connor asked suddenly, catching Jordan by surprise.

'What?'

'Megan. You're always talking about her. Now you're more interested in her than arguing about Sunderland tactics, so that tells me you really like her,' Connor grinned.

'Another time, maybe.'

'I don't get it. I've seen you in some of the Sunderland youth games and you're fearless when a striker is racing towards you for a one-on-one. When you compare it to that, what's so scary about talking to a girl?!'

Jordan smiled. He knew Connor was right. 'I'm just waiting for the right moment,' he replied. 'Now, let's hear your tactics for the Sunderland game.'

Later that week, Jordan was finally brave enough to talk to Megan. They had been at a party together before and at least knew each other's name. But that was it.

Now was the time to change all that, and Jordan had the perfect conversation starter.

'Hi Megan,' he called, walking over to her locker. 'How are things?'

She turned and smiled the prettiest smile. 'Hi Jordan. Ouch, what happened to your eye?'

He shrugged his shoulders. 'It's a story of true bravery,' he replied, grinning. 'Just kidding, I got elbowed at football last night. It looks worse than it is.'

Megan laughed. 'That's it? I thought maybe you'd saved an old lady or stopped a fight.'

'Would that have got me more sympathy?'

'Well, being a goalkeeper is hard work too. I'm always nervous for the keeper. It's so easy for them to get the blame.'

'Tell me about it!' Jordan replied. 'I didn't know you were a football fan.'

'Sunderland all the way,' Megan said. 'I heard you're training at their academy. That must be amazing.'

Jordan tried to play it cool. 'It is. I've got a long

way to go but I think I have a chance of making it to the first team. Maybe you'll be able to come and watch me play one day!'

Megan smiled, 'I'd like that.'

'Okay, well have a nice night. See you tomorrow.' Jordan waved as he walked back towards his locker. Halfway there, he stopped and walked back. It was time to be fearless.

'Megan, there was something else I wanted to ask you,' he said. 'Do you want to see a film together at the weekend? There are some good ones on at the moment.'

Megan didn't answer at first. Jordan watched her thinking about it. 'Hmmm, going to see a film? With you?'

Jordan's heart was beating fast. 'Erm, yes,' he mumbled. 'Only if you want to.' This was starting to feel embarrassing.

Then Megan started giggling. 'I'm just teasing. I wanted to see you sweat a bit. Yes, I'd love to go with you.'

Jordan laughed too. 'Oh come on, what are you

trying to do to me? I was getting ready to dig a hole and disappear!'

Megan took out a pen and wrote down her number. 'Just tell me what time and I'll get my dad to drop me off in town.'

'Sounds great!'

When Jordan got home, he called Connor and excitedly told him the news. 'Do I get an assist for pushing you to finally ask her out?' Connor replied. 'Only you could get elbowed in the eye and yet turn it into a positive thing!'

Jordan laughed. He couldn't wait for the weekend.

They agreed on seeing *The Dark Knight* on Sunday afternoon. When getting ready to go, Jordan tried on four different shirts before deciding that the first one looked best.

They picked up the tickets and then Megan asked, 'Do you want popcorn or some sweets?'

Jordan shook his head, with a sad look on his face. 'I'm on a strict professional diet at Sunderland.'

'Rubbish,' Megan said, hitting his arm playfully. 'I see you eating crisps and chocolate all the time.'

Jordan laughed. 'I should have known you wouldn't fall for that! Let's get popcorn. I'm really hungry.'

After the film, they walked around the little arcade connected to the cinema, and Jordan won Megan a little teddy on a basketball game. They bought drinks, sat at a table in the corner and talked about their families, school stuff and other interests.

Jordan would have happily sat there all day but Megan finally looked at her phone and sighed. 'I've got to go, Jordan,' she said. 'My dad will be waiting outside.'

He walked her to the door. 'Today was really fun,' Megan said. 'Let's do it again soon.'

Jordan grinned. 'I'd like that. See you tomorrow.'

Before she turned to leave, Megan went up on tiptoes and kissed Jordan on the cheek. 'Bye,' she said, and then she was gone.

Jordan stood there for a minute, in shock and feeling his cheeks turning bright red. Then he smiled. It had been the perfect afternoon.

'The first of many, I hope,' he said quietly to himself as he walked back to the bus stop.

CHAPTER 6

CONFIDENT CHARACTER

Jordan wasn't lying to impress Megan; he really did have a good chance of making it in the Sunderland first team. At least, that's what the club's academy coach, Mark Prudhoe, told him.

'If you keep this up, you could be the next Sørensen!'

Jordan wasn't a giant like a lot of keepers, but he had a great leap and long, strong arms. Just when it looked like the ball was flying over his head and into the top corner, he would somehow get his fingertips to it. *Saved!*

'How on earth did you reach that, Picky?' his teammate Billy Knott asked with his hands on his head. He was so sure that he had finally scored against his friend.

Jordan shrugged and smiled. 'Sorry, you're not getting past me today. You might as well give up now!'

Not only did he have great reflexes, but he was also brilliantly brave. When a striker rushed towards him, Jordan spread himself as wide as possible like a starfish. That way, it was almost impossible to score. He had learnt that technique from watching hours and hours of videos of the Manchester United legend, Peter Schmeichel.

Like his hero, Jordan would use any part of his body to keep the ball out of his net – his chest, his legs, even his face if he had to. It was all worth it for a clean sheet!

'How many fingers am I holding up?' Mark Prudhoe asked to make sure that his keeper wasn't concussed.

'Two,' Jordan replied with a cheeky grin, 'which is two more than the number of goals I've conceded today!'

Shot-stopping, however, was only one part of a goalkeeper's game. In modern football, they were expected to do a lot more. Jordan was the last line of the Sunderland defence, but he was also the first line of their attack.

'On my head, Picky!' the strikers would cry out.

Jordan could blast the ball really, really far upfield. Sometimes, his long kicks set up goals, but sometimes, they sailed straight out for a throw-in.

'What was that? Who were you aiming for?' Mark often asked.

But rather than launching it long, Jordan preferred to play out from the back. His striker days at Sir Robert of Newminster Catholic School had made him very comfortable on the ball, and Mark often let him play out-field in training at Sunderland to get extra practice. Jordan loved to dribble past his teammates with Cruyff turns and Zidane roulettes. He even played at left-back a few times in friendly games.

'Please don't try that stuff when you're in goal!' Mark always begged.

In proper matches, Jordan tried not to take too

many risks in between the posts, but he certainly
didn't shy away on his line. He was always talking to
his teammates and calling for the ball. He wanted to
be involved in the match as much as possible.

'If in doubt, play it back!' he shouted to his
defenders. When it came to him, he calmly took a
touch and then found a perfect pass to lead his team
forward.

'Nice one, Picky!' the other players cheered
whenever he set up a goal. More and more of
Sunderland's scoring chances could be traced back
to his boot.

Jordan was a confident character, both on and
off the pitch. One day, his family found a photo of
a five-year-old Jordan standing next to one of his
Sunderland heroes, Kevin Ball. Kevin was now
running the club's academy and Jordan couldn't
wait to show it to him.

'Do you recognise anyone?' he asked cheekily.

Kevin was ready with a clever comeback: 'Well,
the handsome one is obviously me, and I'm guessing
that scrawny little kid is you?'

For once, Jordan was speechless.

Over the years, the Sunderland academy coaches did a good job of making sure that Jordan didn't get too big for his boots.

'You're not the best yet,' Kevin warned when Jordan asked why Steve Bruce wasn't picking him for the first team yet. 'Unless you improve your attitude, you won't make it to the top.'

'I bet I will!' Jordan replied, rising to the challenge. By working harder than ever, he would prove his coach wrong.

He wasn't the finished article yet, though. When things went well, Jordan was Sunderland's super sweeper keeper. When things went wrong, however, it wasn't pretty. There was nothing he liked less than losing. He hated it!

After one particularly bad performance, Jordan just kept kicking his goalposts again and again. He was furious with himself. How had he let such an easy goal in? In the end, his mum had to go over and tell him to stop.

'Come on, you're too old for these tantrums now!'

she told him sternly. 'We all get things wrong – that's how we learn and improve.'

Once he had calmed down, Jordan thought long and hard about his mum's message. She was right, and it was exactly what Mark and Kevin had been saying to him for years. It was good to be competitive, but he couldn't get so angry whenever he made an error – otherwise, as a goalkeeper, he would be angry all the time!

'The best keepers know when to keep calm,' Mark told him. 'They make mistakes, and then they move straight on.'

Yes, Jordan was a winner, but he still had to learn to lose. Disappointment was a big part of football, especially at the highest level. As he got closer and closer to the Sunderland first team, he had to find a better way to bounce back and stay strong. He would need plenty of resilience for the long journey ahead.

CHAPTER 7

WORLD CUP WOBBLE

Word of Jordan's great goalkeeping soon spread beyond Sunderland. The national youth coaches were impressed with his confident style too.

Jordan was over the moon when he got his first call-up to the England Under-16s. It was a dream come true to represent his country at any level. If he kept progressing through the age groups, he could one day become the senior Number 1.

'Hey, you're the new David Seaman!' his Sunderland teammates teased.

Jordan smiled, 'No way, I'm going to be better than him. I would definitely have saved that Ronaldinho free kick at World Cup 2002!'

He could still remember watching that match on a big screen at primary school, aged eight. Even back then, he was already focused on becoming a top goalkeeper.

After five games for the Under-16s, Jordan was called up to the England squad for the 2011 FIFA Under-17 World Cup.

'Mam, I'm off to Mexico!' he cheered, racing around the family home.

Jordan had never been so excited about anything in his life. It was going to be an amazing adventure and his biggest test yet. He would be one vs one with the best young attackers in the world.

'Neymar played in 2009,' Jordan told his teammates, 'and Eden Hazard played in 2007!'

No problem! England's 2011 Under-17 team feared no-one – not Brazil, not Germany, not France, not Argentina.

And why should they? Raheem Sterling and Nathan Redmond were their stars in attack, Nathaniel Chalobah was their captain in the middle, and Jordan was their sweeper keeper extraordinaire. The head coach John Peacock had given him the Number 1 shirt, ahead of Ben Garratt and Tyrell Belford.

'Thanks, you won't regret it!' Jordan assured him.

With a 2–0 win against Rwanda, the Under-17 England team got off to a great start. Jordan didn't have much to do in goal, but he still had to concentrate for the clean sheet.

'Well done, lads!' he cheered at the final whistle. 'More of that please!'

Playing at his first major international tournament, Jordan was feeling confident. Too confident, it turned out. In the second match against Canada, he made World Cup history for entirely the wrong reason.

With five minutes to go, England were 2–1 up and defending well. When Canada won a free kick inside their own half, their keeper Quillan Roberts pushed his players up the pitch.

'Go long!' he shouted. *Bang!*

As a confident character, Jordan didn't like to stay on his line. So, he was out on the edge of his six-yard box as the ball travelled through the air towards his penalty area...

The England centre-back jumped for the header, but he missed it, and so did the Canadian striker. It was only as the ball bounced down in the box that Jordan began to panic. Oh no, it was going over his head! He jumped up and flailed his arms, but he couldn't reach it. 2–2!

Jordan lay down on the grass, trying to make sense of what had just happened. Canada's keeper had just scored a goal against him. What a blunder!

'Oh boy, I'm going to get so much stick for that!' he thought to himself.

His World Cup wobble became world-famous. It was the first time a goalkeeper had ever scored a goal in a FIFA competition. Ever! It was really embarrassing for Jordan, but he couldn't let it get to him. He had to keep his cool. He apologised to his teammates and moved on to focus on the next match.

'Don't worry, that won't ever happen again!' he promised.

As the World Cup went on, Jordan more than made up for that mistake. He kept a clean sheet against Uruguay and then saved the day in the Round of sixteen against Argentina. When the game went to penalties, England needed a hero!

Jordan bounced up and down on his goal line, daring anyone to beat him. The first two takers did, but:

Gaspar Iñíguez tried and failed... *Saved!*

Agustín Allione aimed for the bottom corner, and he guessed the right way... *Saved!*

Jordan sprang to his feet and punched the air.

Moments later, Nathaniel scored to take England into the World Cup quarter-finals!

'Get in!' Jordan and Nathaniel hugged each other, and the rest of the team raced over to join their two heroes.

It was a moment, and a tournament, that Jordan would never ever forget. Even though they lost to Germany in the next round, he went home to Sunderland with his head held high. One day, hopefully, Jordan would get to be England's World Cup hero again.

CHAPTER 8

THE DEEP END AT DARLINGTON

As the Sunderland training session came to an end, Jordan picked up three cones and called to Mark.

'Can we stick around for a few more shots?'

Mark smiled. He had coached Jordan for long enough to know that his young goalkeeper was never in a rush to leave. Some days, Jordan wanted to do extra shot-stopping; other days it was crossing drills. But for once that morning Mark had to say no.

'Actually, Kevin wants a quick chat with you once you've showered and changed.'

Jordan raised his eyebrows. It sounded like something important, but he couldn't tell from Mark's face whether to be worried or excited.

'Really? Any idea what it's about?'

Mark dodged the question. 'The quicker you get over there, the sooner you'll find out.'

Jordan got ready in a hurry. His stomach was wobbling all over the place. He put his bag over his shoulder and stopped in front of the mirror. He didn't want to look scruffy in front of Kevin.

Mark looked over. 'Ready to go?'

Jordan nodded.

When they got to Kevin's office, he was on the phone, but he waved them in anyway. The academy director finished his call and then turned to greet them with a big smile on his face.

'Hey, don't look so worried, Jordan,' he said, reaching over to pat him on the shoulder.

Phew! Jordan relaxed instantly. Those words told him that he wasn't in trouble.

'Have a seat, guys,' Kevin said. 'I'll get straight to the point. I had a call from Darlington this morning. They're having a really rough time at the moment – especially with goalkeepers. They need to get a keeper on loan for the rest of the season. We've offered to help out and we think it would be a great opportunity for you, Jordan.'

Jordan grinned, mainly because he wasn't sure how else to react. He loved Sunderland and working with the youth team coaches, but perhaps it was time for a tougher challenge. Youth football was becoming a little too comfortable for him. This loan move to Darlington would mean playing in the Conference Premier, the fifth division of English football. It would mean testing himself at a higher level against players with lots more experience.

'It'll be a big change,' Kevin said. 'I want you to go into this with your eyes wide open. It's a physical league and the players won't go easy on a seventeen-year-old. They'll think they can push you around.'

'I can handle that,' Jordan replied confidently. 'Do you think I'll have a chance to play, or is it more of a back-up role?'

'Oh no – you'll be the Number 1 from day one. When I said Darlington's situation was tricky, I really meant it! Right now, they don't have a single goalkeeper. We're doing them a big favour, but it'll be worth it if it helps you take the next step on your journey.'

Wow! Jordan liked the sound of that.

'We know what you can do at youth level,' Mark added. 'You're the best keeper in the Under-18s league and we don't want you to get bored. This will be great for your development and we'll be keeping a close eye on you.'

'Any other questions?' Kevin asked.

'Erm... when do they want me there? For training later this week?'

'Ah right. Glad you reminded me on that because that's the other important thing. They need you there for a game tonight!'

Jordan sat forward in his chair. 'Tonight? Wow, okay – well, I better get going then.'

'Craig Liddle is the Darlington manager and he's a good guy. Just ask for him when you get there, and he'll introduce you to the lads.'

He reached over and shook Jordan's hand. 'Good luck! You're going to be terrific.'

As Mark and Jordan walked back towards the car park, there was a long silence.

'Are you okay with all this?' Mark asked. 'Like I said in there, this doesn't change the fact that we see you as a big part of the future here. This will just make you stronger and ready for that moment when it gets here.'

Jordan nodded. 'Yeah, I'm fine. I'm a bit nervous, and a bit excited. There's a lot happening all at once, but by the time I get there tonight I'll be ready.'

'Good lad! Drive safe and we'll call Darlington now to make sure everything is set up for you.'

As Jordan drove out of the car park, his head was still spinning. He had time to rush home, swap his dirty shirt and shorts for fresh ones, and give his mum the short version of the story.

'What a day!' his mum replied, sitting down and rubbing her forehead. 'I guess these things happen quickly in football. Good luck tonight. I'll call your dad and we'll do our best to make it tonight. Darlington is less than an hour away, so we should be fine. Can we spread the word to the rest of the family?'

'Sure, it'll be nice to have a few friendly faces there,' Jordan replied, though he wasn't sure if he meant that. If Darlington were struggling, they might all see him letting in a lot of goals.

By the time he arrived at Darlington's stadium, Jordan had pumped himself up for the biggest game of his career. Craig was sitting on a bench in the car park and greeted him with a big wave and handshake.

'Welcome to Darlington,' he said proudly. 'You have no idea how relieved I am to see you! As Kevin probably said, we're having a bit of a nightmare at the moment.'

Even though Darlington were in the Conference, the dressing room looked good – better than a lot of the places Jordan had played with the Sunderland Under 18s. He heard noise coming from the corridor and a few of the players walked in.

'Is this your son, Craig?' one of them joked.

'Ignore them,' Craig replied, chuckling. 'They're

a good bunch really. I'll introduce you to Tommy Smith and Graeme Lee – you'll be in good hands with them.'

'Welcome to the circus,' Graeme laughed, patting Jordan on the shoulder. 'Last night, I thought I might have to go in goal myself, so we're all happy to see you today!'

'Yeah, nobody wants to see Graeme with the gloves on, trust me,' Tommy added. 'Follow me and we'll go and check that your kit is ready.'

As the clock in the dressing room ticked round to six o'clock, Craig re-appeared. All the players were there now, and he did another quick introduction for Jordan. Jordan gave a shy little wave. He had decided to keep quiet at first until he got a better feel for who the team jokers were. Out on the pitch, however, he knew he would have to be willing to shout at any of his new teammates, even if some were ten, even fifteen, years older than him.

Jordan felt calm during the warm-up and got to know a couple of the substitutes as they took shots at him. But the usual butterflies were there in his stomach at 7:30pm, as he walked down the tunnel and out onto the pitch as a Darlington player for the first time, to face Fleetwood Town.

It wasn't quite how Jordan had imagined making his senior football debut. At The Stadium of Light, Sunderland played in front of 40,000 people every week. This wasn't the Premier League, though. On a cold January night in the Conference, there were just 6,000 brave supporters in The Darlington Arena. Still, they were making plenty of noise:

'Come on, Darlo!'

Just before kick-off, Craig walked round behind Jordan's goal. 'Give it your best, Jordan. In this league, guys are going to try to get under your skin and put you off. Just ignore all the chatter and you'll be fine.'

Jordan was halfway through guzzling from his water bottle, so he just gave Craig a quick thumbs-up. He was ready to be thrown in at the deep end.

Despite all the stories about Darlington conceding three or four goals a game, it was a tight match. Jordan showed his bravery from the very start, rushing out to grab the ball at the edge of his box, just in front of a Fleetwood striker.

'Yes, lad!' the Darlington fans cheered.

As Craig had predicted, Fleetwood tried to put Jordan off whenever they could. From one corner, a tall defender came and stood right in front of Jordan, basically stepping on his toes. Jordan brushed him aside to get a better position.

'Swing it in under the bar,' the defender called out to the corner taker. 'The keeper is five feet tall. He's got no chance!'

'We'll see about that!' Jordan thought to himself. He was determined to prove him wrong. As the ball came in, he quickly stepped in front of the defender and punched the ball clear.

'Well done, keeper!' he heard Graeme call as everyone raced out of the box.

Despite Jordan's safe hands and powerful goal kicks, Darlington were soon under pressure again.

'Push up,' he shouted to his defenders, but they kept getting deeper and deeper. In the second half, a headed clearance bounced up nicely on the edge of the box and a Fleetwood midfielder caught the shot perfectly. Thankfully, Jordan saw it all the way. He dived high to his left and tipped it away for a corner. *Saved!*

'Well done, Jordan!' he heard from a few different voices. He looked up to see his parents clapping on the touchline to his right. He gave them a quick wave as he wiped the mud off his gloves.

Finally, Fleetwood got their goal, but Jordan and his defenders were sure that it was offside. Graeme sprinted over to the assistant referee, waving his arms.

'How can you not see that?' he asked angrily. 'He was miles off!'

As the players limped off towards the dressing room, Jordan was disappointed. He had played well but the result was still the same – another loss for Darlington.

'Heads up, lads,' Craig said, stopping to pat each player on the back. 'One bad decision cost us tonight but we gave it everything. That was our best performance in weeks. If we keep playing like this, we can get back on track.'

After a long pause, Tommy called out, 'Great debut, Jordan! You kept us in it. You didn't deserve to be on the losing team tonight.'

'Thanks, Tommy. We'll win the next one!'

CHAPTER 9

LEARNING TO LOSE

Jordan thought he had learned a lot during his first game for Darlington, but he soon had an even bigger learning experience. Perhaps it was overconfidence after his strong start against Fleetwood – or perhaps he was just off his game, but against Hayes and Yeading, he had a first half to forget.

Early on, their striker Julian Owusu chased after a through-ball, leaving Jordan with a big decision to make. Should he stay on his line or rush out to beat him to the ball? He only had a split second to make up his mind.

Jordan went with his gut instinct and chose to be brave and bold. Out he rushed but, as he slid in for the tackle, he knew he was too late. Foul! The referee had no choice but to point to the spot.

'No, no, no!' Jordan groaned, pounding the grass with his fist.

What an awful mistake! He did his best to save the penalty, but he couldn't quite reach it. 1–0!

'Right,' Jordan thought to himself, 'I really need to make up for that now!'

But minutes later, things got even worse for him. He caught a cross but, in his rush to start an attack, he threw the ball straight to the Hayes and Yeading winger, who raced in and scored. 2–0!

'NO, NO, NO!'

Jordan lay on the ground after the second goal and put his hands on his head. What was he doing? He was a boy amongst men! The crowd was small enough for him to hear every rude word that the angry fans were shouting at him. He had let Darlington down badly and he just wanted to run away and hide.

But no, he couldn't do that. He was a confident character and he had to stay that way. He had to keep his calm and bounce back. Otherwise, things might get *even* worse. Graeme quickly pulled him up and patted him on the arm. 'Chin up! These things happen.'

The match ended in a 3–2 defeat and Jordan blamed no-one but himself. He had stared at the floor in the dressing room at half-time and he was doing the same as the players headed for the showers after the match. He just wasn't used to making big mistakes and he didn't want to talk to anyone.

Once the dressing room was quieter, Craig came over and sat next to him.

'Every great keeper has a tough game like that, Jordan,' he explained. 'You just have to have a short memory. Reset and forget. There's never anything you can do after letting in goals like that, except move forward and focus on the next shot.'

Jordan nodded. 'Thanks, Coach. I will!'

There were plenty more ups and downs during Jordan's season at Darlington. Every week was a new challenge and a new chance to be a hero. After a bad mistake against Telford, he bounced back to finally grab his first clean sheet against Grimsby. When the final whistle blew, he celebrated like he had won the Premier League.

There were a lot more downs than ups, however. He conceded eleven goals in his first five matches in the Number 1 jersey. In total, Jordan played seventeen games during the 2011–12 season, one for each year of his young life. Sadly, he didn't win a single one of them.

'I've almost forgotten how good it feels to win!' Jordan joked with his brother, Richard.

During his time at Darlington, Jordan was certainly learning how to lose, but that was only one of many lessons. He was also learning:

how to push his way past strong strikers to catch crosses,

how to decide when to play safe and when to be bold,

how to kick the ball powerfully *and* accurately,

how to stay focused for the full ninety minutes,

and how to bark out instructions, even to teammates twice his age!

Sadly, Jordan's many super saves weren't enough to lift Darlington off the bottom of the table and, eventually, they were relegated. With a heavy heart, Jordan said his goodbyes.

'Thanks for everything, Picky!' the fans cheered.

'Without you, we would have been down months ago,' his teammates told him. 'You're going to be a top keeper one of these days!'

His manager Craig gave him a big hug before he got in his car. 'You should be very proud of what you've done here, lad. It takes real guts to fight like that at your age. I always knew you were a special talent, even when I coached you in the Sunderland Under-12s, but you've surprised even me. Keep it up and the future's yours!'

Jordan had done his very best to rescue 'Darlo'. He would miss everyone at the club, but it was time to head back to Sunderland and find out what his next adventure would be.

CHAPTER 10

AMAZING AT ALFRETON

From the deep end at Darlington, Jordan returned to Sunderland as a more resilient character, as well as a better goalkeeper. The testing times had really helped to toughen him up. He felt ready for more first-team experience, but did the youth coaches agree?

It was a little strange to report back to the academy after an eventful six months away. Jordan felt like so much had changed but he was looking forward to catching up with his old teammates again.

'You survived, Picky!' they teased. 'We didn't think you'd cope with conceding that many goals.'

Jordan laughed, 'Neither did I, but it makes every save taste a whole lot sweeter!'

Kevin was pleased to have his confident keeper back. 'You did a great job at Darlo, Jordan,' he said when they sat down for a quick chat before the 2012–13 campaign. 'I've never seen Craig so impressed! The plan for this season is to get you some Under-18s games to start with, and then find you another loan move to get you more competitive game-time.'

Jordan nodded. 'Sounds good to me.'

Jordan was as dominant as ever in training and helped his team get off to a great start in the youth league. But he was always thinking about when and where his next loan move might be. Perhaps this time he would get to play in League Two, or League One, or even the Championship!

When Mark called him over before training one February morning, Jordan knew straight away that they had found a team. With butterflies in his stomach, he jogged over.

'Ready to go back to getting knocked around by grown men?' Mark asked, with a smile. 'We've set up a loan deal with Alfreton Town.'

Jordan tried but failed to hide his disappointment. He was heading back to the Conference Premier again.

'Okay, when do they want me?' he asked.

Mark paused. He had known Jordan for long enough to know that this wasn't quite the news he had dreamed of.

'We've agreed that you'll join them for training at some point later this week and then you may well be starting on Saturday. Look, I know you'd have loved to get some experience in a higher league. We made lots of calls, but this is the best situation available at the moment.'

'Don't worry, I'll have more of a smile on my face by the time I get there!' Jordan said. 'It's still a great chance to show what I can do.'

After his time at Darlington, he knew what to expect. Nicky Law, the Alfreton Town manager, gave him a warm welcome. 'We're delighted to have you. We've got a good group of lads, and a few of them are youngsters on loan like you.'

Nicky introduced him to Aden Flint, another

recent addition to the Alfreton Town squad.

'You'll enjoy it here,' Aden said, after Nicky had left. 'A lot of the older guys work part-time on the side, just so they can keep playing football. They really care about this club!'

'Yeah, it makes you think, doesn't it?' Jordan replied. 'We're just here to listen and learn, but it's a different situation for the older players with bills to pay.'

Before long, Jordan was very glad that Sunderland had done the deal with Alfreton Town. He enjoyed the training sessions and picked up lots of tips from Nicky. As promised, Jordan was the first-choice keeper from the start. On his debut against Hyde, he didn't quite get the clean sheet he wanted, but his kicking helped Alfreton to a 5–1 thrashing.

'I've won a game already!' Jordan cheered, throwing his arms up in the air like a champion.

He felt on top of the world, and that feeling continued in the next game against Wrexham. It was 1–1 with seconds to go when their striker Dele Adebola fired a powerful shot at goal. BANG!

Jordan watched it carefully as it flew towards him.

'I've got this!' he told himself.

He leapt up and tipped the ball over the crossbar...

Saved!

The Alfreton fans went wild for their new young hero, and so did the players. After the final whistle, his teammates ran over to thank their man of the match.

'What an incredible stop – we owe you big-time, Picky!'

Soon enough, Jordan had that precious first clean sheet he was looking for. It was all going so well, and Nicky was delighted for him.

'He's a bright lad and he has got a big, big future ahead of him,' the Alfreton Town manager told the media.

Jordan was loving every minute of his time at the club. What a way to learn! Playing against men week in week out, he was getting better and better, and making fewer and fewer mistakes. He wasn't the perfect keeper yet, though.

Against Lincoln City, Jordan was on fire. He made save after save after save to keep his team in the game. With ten minutes to go, Alfreton were only 1–0 down.

'Come on, we can still grab a point here!' he shouted from his goal.

But when Jordan came out to catch the ball, Lincoln's giant striker jumped up and headed it past him into the empty net. 2–0!

It was another nightmare moment and the old Jordan would have kicked his goalposts in anger. But the new Jordan just gave a little smile. After all, it was nowhere near as embarrassing as that Canada goal! Bad things happened to keepers, but great things happened too. He couldn't win every time.

The three months at Alfreton flew by. Before he knew it, Jordan was back at Sunderland, wondering 'What's next?'

Nicky tried to sign him on a permanent deal, but The Black Cats said, 'No, Pickford's our future number one!'

CHAPTER 11

ON THE MOVE AGAIN

One thing was crystal clear for Jordan: he wanted to keep playing against men week in week out, rather than returning to the youth leagues, or sitting on the bench at Sunderland. In the first team, he was still a long way behind the two top keepers, Keiren Westwood and Vito Mannone.

'If you can find me another loan deal, I'd love to do it,' Jordan told Mark and Kevin that summer. 'I learned so much from my time at Darlington and Alfreton Town.'

'We'll see what we can do,' Kevin replied. 'Our main focus is getting you ready to take over here at Sunderland. It's still a little soon for that, but we want to give you every chance to learn at the professional level. You're the number three keeper here at the moment. That's going to change quickly if you keep playing so well, but for now regular game-time is the best way to help you develop.'

Jordan smiled. 'Great. Well, I'll be working hard all summer so I'm ready for whatever lies ahead in August.'

'Give yourself a break!' Mark said. 'Take Megan away somewhere and sit on a beach. There will be plenty of time to be in the gym in July.'

Jordan took Mark's advice but kept an eye on his phone. He jumped up from his chair when he saw Kevin's number appear on the screen one morning in early July.

'Hi Jordan,' Kevin said. 'I thought you'd like to know that we've set you up with Burton Albion for this season. That's a club on the rise.'

'Perfect, thanks!' Jordan replied. Hurray, he was moving up to League Two!

'One thing to think about – and we can talk more on this – is that you'll need to move down there.

I'm sure we can work with Burton to get you a temporary place. Their boss, Gary Rowett, is a top man and a really good manager. From everything I've heard, you'll love playing for him.'

Jordan was silent for a minute as he thought about moving away from home – away from his parents and away from Megan. He had been lucky not to have to do that for the other loan spells.

'Still there, Jordan?'

'Yes, just thinking it all through.'

'We'll be keeping a close eye on things. Like we said, regular playing time is the key but if we get an injury at Sunderland, the boss may bring you back.'

Sadly, it was an injury of his own that first brought Jordan back to Sunderland. After only a few games in goal for Burton, he returned to have treatment on his knee.

'It's nice to come home!' he admitted. Moving away from his friends and family was proving harder than he had expected.

However, Jordan didn't give up. Once his knee

was feeling better, he went back to Burton and this time, he made sure that he settled in.

'Stay, we need you here!' Gary told him.

Burton were on a losing run, but Jordan's safe hands helped to turn their fortunes around. He produced a string of super saves as they won at Wycombe Wanderers, Chesterfield and Exeter City.

'See, I told you we need you!' Gary laughed.

The Burton manager helped Jordan in lots of ways, especially improving his communication with his defenders. The more he talked to the back four and pointed out things that they might not have spotted, the easier the game became. Gary encouraged him to use his feet too and play as a sweeper to collect through-balls.

'Sure thing!' Jordan said happily.

He was enjoying himself as Burton's new Number 1. It was great to get real first-team experience and The Brewers were even challenging for promotion. Plus, he didn't feel so homesick now that he was sharing a flat with Adam Reed, his old friend from Sunderland.

84

However, just as Jordan was getting comfortable, he was on the move back to Sunderland. Keiren had injured his shoulder and the manager Gus Poyet needed a back-up for Vito.

'I'm on my way!' Jordan told them, quickly packing his bags.

For eleven Premier League games in late 2013 and early 2014, he sat on the Sunderland bench, ready and waiting to put on the gloves and play. In the end, Jordan wasn't needed but it did give him a chance to study top-level football up close. He got to work with Vito in training, and he got to watch Chelsea's Petr Čech and Tottenham's Hugo Lloris in action.

'That's going to be me soon!' Jordan kept telling himself. His self-belief was as strong as ever.

Once Keiren recovered, Jordan was free to head out on loan again. He didn't go back to Burton, though. Gary tried to persuade him, but Jordan had received a better offer. League One side Carlisle United needed a new keeper to help them fight relegation.

'I'm on my way!' Jordan told them, quickly packing his bags.

Although it started out as a one-month loan, Jordan pushed his way past the two other keepers to claim the Number 1 shirt and stayed until the end of the season.

'You're a class act, kid,' the Carlisle manager Graham Kavanagh said when it was time for Jordan to leave. 'We were lucky to have you!'

At the end of the 2013–14 season, after a mad year on the move, Jordan couldn't wait to settle back at Sunderland for the summer. There was even a nice present waiting for him, a reward for all his hard work and dedication – a big new four-year contract!

CHAPTER 12

BRAVERY AT BRADFORD

Jordan wasn't staying put at Sunderland, though. Not yet anyway. There were still two experienced keepers in front of him at the club. But with his big new contract, he was happy to wait and build up his experience elsewhere. He had already played in the Conference Premier and League Two, but what was next? League One? The Championship?

Jordan just wanted to keep playing. As the 2014–15 season kicked off, he was only twenty and he knew there was only so much he could learn as a third-choice keeper playing in the reserves. So, when Bradford City came calling, he jumped at the chance.

'I'm on my way!' Jordan told them, quickly packing his bags.

From the minute he arrived at Valley Parade, he knew this would be a step-up from his other loan spells. Not only would he be playing League One football, but he would be playing in front of 25,000 fans each week.

'To be honest, we're taking a bit of a gamble here, Jordan,' explained Phil Parkinson, the Bradford boss. 'The fans have high expectations here, but just focus on your game and you'll be great! We've seen what you can do and we're so pleased to have you here.'

He called Megan from his hotel room. 'This is going to be a strong season – I can feel it! Everyone is really friendly here and the stadium is a lot bigger than the other places I've played. Plus, we're going to be chasing promotion, so every game will really count.'

'That's amazing, hun. Like you always say, it's all part of the journey.'

But it would be a testing time too, with a rough start.

Jordan was fired up as he walked out to face Coventry. He wanted to show his new club Bradford what he could do. With his first few touches, he was quick to send the ball far downfield.

'You can kick it a mile. When you get the chance, try to set the strikers free with a quick long ball,' Phil had told him in training that week.

Bradford were 1–0 up and Jordan was starting to feel confident. Too confident, it turned out. As a corner came in from the right, he thought he had a chance of either catching it or punching it away. But there were too many bodies in the way and he was one step too slow in coming off his line. He went flying out to the ball, but a tall defender beat him to it, heading it easily into the empty net. Jordan was left lying on the ground as the Coventry players celebrated. What a schoolboy error!

'No, no, NO!' he groaned, clapping his gloves together angrily.

Why had he done that? Jordan didn't need to come rushing out. He would have saved the header if he had just stayed on his line. As he replayed the

goal in his mind, Coventry struck again. He made
a good save on a low shot, but he could only push
the ball straight to a Coventry player for a tap-in. He
slapped the ground as he got up. It was turning into
a nightmare afternoon.

Bradford fought back to win, but there was
plenty of attention on Jordan's performance after
the game. He knew he would have to play better.
He thought back to some of his low points at
Darlington, at Burton Albion, at the Under-17
World Cup. The best goalkeepers were the ones
who could learn from their mistakes and then put
those disappointments aside.

Jordan was due to go to a charity event that
evening to support the club. When Phil asked if he
still felt like going, Jordan raised his eyebrows. 'Of
course, I'll just make sure I wear my thickest jumper
in case people start throwing stuff at me!'

Phil smiled at him, and went back to his office,
where one of the other coaches asked him about
Jordan and whether they might give the backup
keeper a chance in the next game.

Phil shook his head: 'From everything I know about Jordan, he's going to be just fine.'

Jordan proved his manager right by getting better and better with every game.

After a 1–0 win, Jordan felt a big slap on the back. He turned to see Phil grinning. 'I don't know how you do it. There were three times today when I was sure they were going to score and then you'd get a hand or foot or shoulder in the way. Incredible stuff.'

Bradford were still fighting for a playoff spot in March 2015 when Jordan's phone buzzed. It was Gus Poyet, the Sunderland manager.

'Listen, we've had an injury setback here and we need you back at Sunderland as cover,' Gus said. 'I've already spoken to Phil and the Bradford chairman, so they know what's going on.'

Jordan was crushed. He was loving his time at Bradford and knew that going back to Sunderland would mean sitting on the bench every weekend. But it was all part of the bigger plan.

'Okay, thanks for the heads up,' he said. 'I'll see you at training.'

As he said his goodbyes to the Bradford players, striker James Hanson appeared with a big cushion with the club badge on it. 'Jordan, this is for you. Just so you don't forget your time here.'

Now Jordan was even sadder about leaving. He was just about to thank them with some emotional speech, when James added, 'Oh and it'll stop your bum hurting when you're sitting on the Sunderland bench!'

They all burst out laughing, even Jordan. 'I knew there was a joke hidden in this somewhere!'

Back at Sunderland, Jordan tried to stay positive. Costel Pantilimon was Gus's first choice for keeper and all Jordan could do was to play his best in training. When he saw Dick Advocaat replace Gus as manager shortly afterwards, Jordan hoped that might be the break he needed, but Dick still picked Costel every week.

'Be patient,' Jordan told himself over and over again. But for how long?

CHAPTER 13

IMPRESSING AT PRESTON

At the start of the 2015–16 season, Dick Advocaat called Jordan to his office for the kind of chat that he was now very used to. Surprise, surprise – another loan move!

'Jordan, we love what you're doing in training,' Dick said. 'It's just that we're expecting to be in a relegation battle again this season and it's a tough time to bring in a young keeper. You've got many great years ahead of you and I hope that most of them will be spent at Sunderland.'

Jordan nodded. He understood the message and he was now more interested in hearing about where he would be playing this season.

'Preston North End are interested, and we think it's a great fit. That'll be your first taste of Championship football and another chance to add to your game.'

Jordan jumped out of his seat to shake Dick's hand. 'That's great news! I'm up for the challenge.'

As Jordan left the office, he felt confident enough to turn around and say, 'Make sure you're watching my games, though. You'll like what you see, I promise!'

The first person that Jordan met when he arrived at Preston was Alan Kelly, his goalkeeper coach. Jordan had heard about Alan's career at Sheffield United and Blackburn.

'I'm going to push you hard, but you'll thank me later,' Alan said. 'I've watched a lot of tape of your games at Bradford and for the Sunderland youth teams. I wouldn't say this if I didn't mean it: you've got all the tools to be one of the best keepers in the game.'

Jordan went bright red. He couldn't think of anything to say at first, and finally managed to reply: 'Thanks, that means a lot.'

'We'll work on everything, but I know you're already a top shot-stopper and you're good with the ball at your feet. I'm more interested in things like positioning and just keeping your mind sharp.'

The Preston manager Simon Grayson was a big fan of Jordan too. 'We've had our eye on you for a while. When we got promoted last season, we felt it was the right time to take a chance and call Sunderland. I really believe you can help us stay in the Championship this season.'

Jordan liked to keep count of his clean sheets, and Preston's defensive game plan gave him good protection. He started the season with a 0–0 draw against Middlesbrough, then made two great saves in a 1–0 win over Milton Keynes Dons. Jordan added two more clean sheets, taking his tally to four by the end of August.

He was growing in confidence with every game, and he hoped Dick was watching. But by October, Dick had resigned with Sunderland in the bottom three and Sam Allardyce had been brought in. Yet again, Jordan was left wondering what this change of management might mean for him.

'Just focus on your football,' his dad told him one night in mid-October. 'Everything else is out of your control.'

It was good advice. Jordan went out and made his own statement, putting together six clean sheets in a row as Preston continued to prove that they could survive in the Championship. Alan and Simon both came over to give him a big hug after a late save in a 0–0 draw against Bolton.

'That's what we brought you here for,' Simon said excitedly. 'There aren't many keepers that would have saved that!'

Just as Jordan was starting to feel settled at Preston, he got another call from Sunderland. Not again! But this time, it was different.

'Hi Jordan,' Sam said. 'You've been doing a great job at Preston and I want you back here, playing for us! It's time to throw you in at the deep end and see if you sink or swim. I want you to get a few games now so that you're ready to take over as first choice next season.'

Jordan almost dropped the phone. The rest of the conversation was a blur. He just remembered himself saying 'yes' a lot and agreeing to be back at training later in the week.

He called Megan. 'I just got the phone call that I've been dreaming about since I was six!'

'You won the lottery?' she teased.

'It feels like that, yes. They want me back at Sunderland and I'm actually going to play!'

'Oh Jordan, that's amazing! I'm so happy for you. I'm relieved too. I keep telling everyone I'm going out with a Sunderland keeper and no-one believes me!'

Jordan laughed. He thought about all his family, his school friends and his teachers. If he finally got his chance at Sunderland, it would be so special for everyone who had supported him over the years.

CHAPTER 14

FINALLY!

It was the first week of January 2016 when Jordan got back to Sunderland, and he met with Sam before catching up with his teammates.

As he found his spot in the dressing room, Lee Cattermole walked in. 'Hello stranger!' he said, giving Jordan a big hug.

'Remind me, what's your name again?' joked John O'Shea. They had got used to seeing Jordan for a few weeks every season in between the loan moves. 'I thought you were on a loan tour of the country still!'

Sam called Jordan over towards the end of training. 'I can already see why everyone rates you so highly. We've got Arsenal in the FA Cup this weekend and I want to freshen things up. You're going to start.'

Jordan wanted to take off his shirt and sprint around the pitch waving it above his head. Instead, he grinned and said, 'Thanks, boss. I won't let you down!'

He couldn't even wait until he got home before spreading the news. Sitting in the players' cafeteria, he picked at a plate of pasta while texting his parents, his brother, Megan and every friend he could think of.

The replies came back quickly, all congratulating him and wishing him good luck. The text from his brother said: 'Well, you've been at Sunderland since you were eight so it's about time! Congrats, pal.'

With Jordan due to travel down to London with the squad on Friday morning, his parents arranged a small party on the Thursday night to mark the moment. Once most people had left, his dad put his arm around Jordan's shoulder.

'I couldn't be happier for you, Jordan. I really couldn't be. You've done it the hard way. I'm sure you'll be nervous but make sure you enjoy it too.'

Jordan woke early on Saturday morning and started going through his usual routine: a few stretches, some water, a few text messages. After that, he had an important phone call to make.

'How are you doing, kid?' his old youth coach Kevin answered. 'Excited about today?'

'You bet, Bally! I just wanted to thank you for everything you've done for me. I know I wasn't always the easiest kid to coach, but I really wouldn't be here without you!'

Kevin chuckled. 'Thanks, Picky, but you've got there through your own hard work. I always hoped this day would come – good luck!'

Jordan joined the team for breakfast and before long they were boarding the coach to the stadium.

'Away to Arsenal in the FA Cup. Not a bad way to start,' John said, patting him on the back. 'I'm chuffed for you. Good luck today.'

When Jordan got the teamsheet, he saw that Arsenal were resting some players too, but it was still a strong side. He had a chance to walk around on the pitch in his tracksuit and then headed into the dressing room. When he walked through the door, he stopped still.

'Seen a ghost?' Lee asked.

But Jordan was just staring at the Sunderland goalkeeper shirt hanging on the far side of the dressing room, with 'Pickford 13' on the back.

'Did they spell it wrong?' Lee joked. 'Go on, it won't bite. Go and take a look.'

Jordan snapped a couple of quick photos while no-one was looking and sent them off to Megan and his family. 'You're always Number 1 for us!' his mum wrote back.

He sat down and looked around the room. It was just another game, eleven vs eleven. But it felt different to every other game he had ever played. He got changed for the warm up and laid out his tape and shin pads, so he wouldn't be rushed when he came back.

He felt good in the warm-up. The ball was hitting his gloves nicely and he was smashing his goal kicks well over the halfway line.

Sam kept the team talk short. 'Look, we've had a rough time in the league. Put that aside. This is the FA Cup. We're not playing for survival today, so let's play with some freedom.'

He had a quiet word for Jordan too as the players headed for the tunnel. 'Just play your game. Go and do what you do best.'

As Jordan walked out onto the pitch for the first time as Sunderland's goalkeeper, it was everything he had dreamed of. He kept looking down at the badge on the left side of his shirt. He had worn plenty of different badges over the past few years, but this was always the one closest to his heart.

Jordan was in action right from the start. Arsenal attacked down the left and he had to react quickly to palm away a low shot. At the other end, Sunderland took a surprise lead. But from then on, it was all Arsenal. They levelled with a low shot that gave Jordan no chance. 1–1!

Theo Walcott tested him moments later, but Jordan dived to tip the ball away... *Saved!*

It was the same story in the second half. Jordan

narrowed the angle expertly to save a one-on-one chance and then reacted quickly for another diving stop... *Saved!*

Arsenal finally scored two close range goals, but Jordan had certainly caught the eye.

'You kept us in it for a long time,' Sam said, patting Jordan on the back.

The dressing room was quiet after another loss, but Jordan believed there was enough talent to get away from the relegation zone.

Jordan was on the bench for the next game as Vito Mannone came back in, but Sam handed him a Premier League debut a week later away at Tottenham. Sunderland lost 4–1 but Jordan again played well, making spectacular saves to deny Harry Kane and Christian Eriksen. Of the goals he conceded, one was deflected, and another was a penalty.

Later that week, Sam pulled him aside for a quick chat. 'Jordan, you've looked right at home playing against Premier League players and I know you've got a bright future here. But I need to tell you we're going to stick with Vito for the rest of the season. I wanted to be honest with you. I'm sorry but we just need a little more experience for the relegation fight ahead.'

That stung. Even though Sam had always said that it was about building towards next season, Jordan had hoped that his saves against Arsenal and Tottenham might change his mind. Apparently not. He nodded but he wasn't sure what else to say.

'You can still get a lot out of this season,' Sam told him. 'Take it all in. Watch the way that John, Lee and the others train. Keep working on your game. You're so nearly there!'

Jordan followed Sam's advice and cheered on his teammates as they narrowly avoided relegation by two points. Phew! Sunderland were staying in the Premier League and Jordan was going to be their new Number 1.

CHAPTER 15

SUNDERLAND'S NUMBER 1

When Jordan heard that Sam Allardyce would not be back as Sunderland manager for the 2016–17 season, his heart sank. Now he would have to do it all over again to impress the new manager, David Moyes.

'Don't give up now,' Megan told him one afternoon. She could see that Jordan was lost in his own thoughts, probably worrying about what would come next.

'I just don't know if I can do another loan spell after having that taste of playing for Sunderland. I'm good enough to start, I know I am.'

'So go and prove it,' Megan replied. 'Make it impossible for them to choose anyone but you.'

Jordan smiled for the first time that day. 'You're right. It's all in my hands.'

'Literally, in your hands!' Megan joked.

Jordan worked hard during preseason training and kept his cool when David decided that Vito would start the season in goal. 'It's okay,' he told his parents one evening. 'I'll win him over eventually!'

Sunderland lost their first two games of the season and, after the whole team watched some clips from their loss to Middlesbrough, David called Jordan up to his office.

Jordan had a horrible feeling that he knew what was coming next: yet another loan move! He could feel some of the frustration bubbling up inside him.

'Have a seat, Jordan,' David said, while moving some papers across his desk. 'Two losses from two games is not the start I was hoping for. That leaves me with some tough decisions to make. Something has to change.'

He paused. Jordan had a slightly confused look on his face. This didn't sound like the usual conversation about going out on loan.

'Vito has picked up an injury and we need to think about the future. You have done everything that this club has asked of you. You've put in the time on loan, improved different areas of your game, and played well in the few games you've had for Sunderland. I think it's time we backed you 100 per cent.'

Jordan's mouth dropped open. 'What are you saying, boss?' he asked.

'I want to give you a proper chance. Not just a game here and a game there. I want you to be my first-choice keeper.'

Jordan's first thought was to jump up and hug David. Those were the words he had been waiting to hear for years from previous Sunderland managers – from Martin O'Neill, then Paolo Di Canio, then Gus Poyet, then Dick Advocaat, then Sam Allardyce...

'I don't know what to say,' Jordan admitted. 'This is the best news I've ever heard. I thought you were about to send me on loan again, so this has turned out better than expected!'

David laughed. 'Sorry to put you through that!

Look, there will be bumps along the way. You're a young keeper taking his first steps in the Premier League. That isn't easy. But I don't want you to play with any kind of fear. I'm not going to take the shirt away from you if you have a few bad games. I believe in you.'

They shook hands and Jordan walked back to the cafeteria. His legs felt like jelly.

'You okay?' Lee asked.

'Yes, fine,' Jordan replied. 'Lots on my mind, that's all.'

Lee looked at him. 'I think I can guess what that's about, but I'll wait until the boss tells us the team later on.'

Jordan tried not to give anything away. He wasn't sure how much he could say yet.

But once David named the team and confirmed that Jordan was starting in goal, he let himself start enjoying the moment.

Vito walked over after the team meeting and Jordan worried about what to say. But there was no reason to panic.

'Congratulations!' Vito said, patting Jordan on the back. 'I wish you all the best. You're going to be a great keeper for a long time.'

For eighty-four minutes, Jordan played brilliantly away at Southampton. He kept his team in the game with three diving super saves.

'Pickford! Pickford!' the Sunderland fans chanted his name.

When Jermain Defoe scored a penalty, Jordan dared to dream of a win and a clean sheet.

'We're nearly there,' he told himself.

But then Jay Rodriguez got the ball outside the Sunderland penalty area and shot through a crowd of defenders. The ball swerved through the air and squirmed just under Jordan's outstretched arms. 1–1!

He pounded the grass with his gloves. How had he let that in? All his hard work was for nothing! As the Saints fans celebrated behind him, there was nowhere for Jordan to hide.

'Sorry lads, I really messed up there,' he said as he trudged back into the dressing room.

During his many loan spells, Jordan had learned

that it was best to hold his hands up and accept his mistakes.

'Forget it, mate,' Jermain told him. 'You were brilliant today!'

Jordan moved on to the next date circled on his calendar. He would finally be making his home debut!

In the days leading up to the game, he tried to get as many tickets as possible for his family, his friends, Megan's family and the list went on. Whatever the result, it was going to be the proudest day of his life.

The night before the game, he hardly slept. At first, he was picturing what might happen in the game and the saves he would make. Then he worried about making a big mistake in front of so many people he knew. After a few hours of sleep, he gave up at 4am and went downstairs to watch TV.

A few minutes later, he heard footsteps on the stairs and his brother Richard appeared. 'This is going to sound weird, but I couldn't sleep because I was excited for you!'

Jordan laughed. 'At least I'm not the only one!'

'Want some toast?' Richard whispered on his way to the kitchen.

'Sure,' Jordan replied.

A few minutes later, Richard was back with toast and two glasses of orange juice. 'I'd be happy to take your mind off things by thrashing you at *FIFA* on the PlayStation... if you think that'll help, I mean'

'Wow, that's big talk. Let's do it.'

Jordan quickly relaxed. He won both games against Richard, though he had some suspicions that his brother was letting him win.

Soon, the whole family was up and a few neighbours were dropping in to wish him luck. Jordan dished out hugs and handshakes, and then left for an 11am team meeting.

By the time he went out for the warm-up, the stadium was filling up. He remembered where his tickets were and he found his own little supporters' club huddled in one corner behind the goal where he was warming up. He gave them a quick wave.

Back in the dressing room, he taped up his ankles and bounced a ball to stay sharp. With just a few minutes to go, he put on his goalkeeper shirt and took a deep breath. He couldn't wait to hear the roar of the Sunderland fans.

Standing in the tunnel, he jumped on the spot and rolled his neck from side to side. 'You can do no wrong,' Lee said, turning to face him. 'The fans love you already!'

He heard the referee call out 'Okay, lads,' and then they were moving down the tunnel and out onto the pitch. The noise was deafening. He saw red and white everywhere, and felt energy pouring through his body.

As they read out the teams over the loudspeaker, he got a loud cheer, especially from one particular corner of the crowd. He grabbed a few last sips of water and got himself fully in the zone. He was ready.

Sunderland were off the pace from the very first whistle. Within seconds, Jordan had to race out to snatch a cross in front of Romelu Lukaku.

'Focus!' he screamed at his teammates. Yes, he was the new kid but he didn't mind raising his voice.

Twenty minutes later, a perfect cross came in from the right and Lukaku sent a powerful header towards the corner. But Jordan had guessed that Lukaku would aim for that corner and he sprung to his left to make a brilliant one-handed stop... *Saved!*

The crowd were on their feet clapping, and there was still time for him to pull off another diving save before half-time. As he jogged off the pitch, he could hear the fans in the front row:

'Great half, Jordan!'

'You're keeping us in this, lad!'

'Terrific saves!'

Sadly, there was nothing Jordan could do in the second half. Lukaku scored a hat-trick of unstoppable goals and boos rang out around the stadium. When the third goal flew into the net, Jordan sat with his hands on his knees. The Premier League could be very cruel.

When he got home, his family did their best to make him feel better.

'You were the only good thing to come out of today,' Richard said. 'Otherwise, it was another rubbish performance!'

'It could have been 4–0 at half-time if you hadn't

made all those saves! Where were your defenders?'
his dad added.

Jordan said nothing. He was pleased with his own
performance, but the loss was painful. It was only
September and there was a long way to go before
the season was over, but things were already looking
shaky for Sunderland.

The losses kept piling up and it was early
November by the time they got their first win of the
season against Bournemouth. Jordan was doing a
sterling job in goal, but his teammates were giving
him too much work to do. He couldn't save the day
every time, but sometimes he did.

At the Stadium of Light, Sunderland were 2–1
up but Leicester City piled on the pressure at the
end. In the final minute of stoppage time, they won
a corner and sent all their big men up from the
back. The cross fell to Wes Morgan, who shot low
towards the bottom corner. It was a strong strike,
but Jordan refused to be beaten again... *Saved!*

'What a hero!' his teammates cheered happily at
the final whistle.

The good times didn't last, though. Another winless run between Christmas and early February left Sunderland with slim survival hopes.

A 4–0 win over Crystal Palace briefly put a smile on Jordan's face but they lost eight of their next ten games as relegation became a certainty.

'I can't believe that after waiting so long for a chance at Sunderland, we're going to get relegated in my first season,' Jordan said one evening after the team's latest disappointing loss. 'It feels like such a failure!'

'Come on, Jordan,' his mum said cheerfully. 'You've got to look at the positives. You've proved yourself in the Premier League! David thought you were the right man for the job and you have kept the team in games all season with your saves. You can't do everything.'

As if to back up his mum's words, Jordan got more proof about his strong season when he was included in England's squad for the Under 21 European Championships that summer in Poland.

'Just carry on doing what you've done all year,'

the England Under-21 team manager Aidy Boothroyd said. 'Can't wait to work with you again.'

Jordan felt the pain of Sunderland's relegation, both as a player and as a fan. He knew so many Sunderland fans and wondered if they thought he had let them down.

'Are you serious?' his friends laughed. 'You were easily one of our stars this season. You were even shortlisted for the PFA Young Player of the Year award!'

Jordan headed off to the Under-21 European Championships in Poland. After that, he would prepare for another season at Sunderland, and try to lead the club back into the Premier League. That was his plan, but he would soon find out that more twists and turns lay ahead.

CHAPTER 16

EVERTON AND THE EUROS

Jordan was just finishing lunch with his England Under-21 teammates when he got the call from his agent. He picked up, wondering what could be so important.

'I just got some big news and I wanted to pass it on. Are you sitting down?'

'Yes, yes, tell me,' he said, getting up from the table and finding a quiet corner. 'You can't just say that and then pause!'

'Everton have made a big offer for you. They want you to be their main keeper, so you might be staying in the Premier League after all! We're still waiting to hear what Sunderland are going to do, but it's a great offer.'

Jordan's head was spinning, but he finally managed to reply. 'Okay, give me some time to think, and let me know if you hear more.'

He put his phone in his pocket and went for a walk. Moving to a club like Everton would be a huge step in his career, but that would mean leaving Sunderland behind. Although he had been out on loan plenty of times before, this was different. This would be the end of his childhood dream.

'Sunderland has always been home to me,' he explained when he called his parents that night. 'I want to help the club get back into the Premier League.'

'Jordan, this is going to sound strange but maybe this is the best way you can help Sunderland get promoted. If they use the money to pay wages and rebuild the squad, you'll have still done your part.'

'I hadn't really thought of it like that,' he replied. 'Everton are a great club too. If the deal goes through, I'm sure I'll be treated well there.'

There was nothing else he could do. It was now

just a waiting game. In the meantime, he had to get ready for the Under-21 European Championships.

'I'll let you know the minute I hear anything,' he told his mum. 'The next time you see me, I might be an Everton player!'

It was hard for Jordan to focus on his training with all the transfer rumours swirling around, so it was a relief for him that things moved quickly. Sunderland accepted the offer and the deal was soon done. £30 million – he was now the world's third-most expensive goalkeeper, and Britain's most expensive ever.

'I've got a lot to live up to now!' Jordan joked with his family. It was a good thing that he was such a confident character.

Of course, it didn't take long for the news to spread around the England camp. Mason Holgate, who was on the fringes of the Everton squad, was the first to congratulate him.

'Great news, big man,' he said, grabbing Jordan in a playful headlock. 'We're building a team for the future!'

'Bring it on!' Jordan cheered.

Aidy knocked on Jordan's door later that day when he heard the news. 'That's terrific, Jordan,' he said. 'I'm chuffed for you. Everton are a great family club.'

Before long, it was time for their first game of the Under-21 tournament against Sweden. As the game kicked off, all eyes were on England's £30 million keeper. Was Jordan really worth all that money? Yes!

With ten minutes to go, their left-back Ben Chilwell slid in for a tackle on the edge of the area. The referee pointed to the spot – penalty to Sweden!

Now, the pressure was really on Jordan. A 0–0 draw would be a decent result for the Three Lions, but a 1–0 defeat would be a disaster.

'You're not getting past me!' Jordan muttered as he bounced up and down on his goal line.

Linus Wahlqvist stepped up and chipped the ball straight down the middle. Jordan just stood tall and batted the ball away... *Saved!*

'Thanks, mate!' Ben said, looking mightily relieved.

Jordan's penalty save filled England with confidence. They went on to beat Slovakia 2–1 and Poland 3–0, as they finished top of the group. Thanks to their goalkeeping hero, they had two clean sheets out of three.

'We've shouldn't be scared of anyone!' Jordan said to Mason as they relaxed at the hotel. 'Germany will be tough in the semi-finals but we're good enough to get through.'

'It would be great for English football if we could bring home a big trophy, even at Under-21 level,' Mason replied.

After the disappointment of relegation, Jordan had worried that he would be miserable at the tournament, but he was loving every minute of it. With all the loan spells, he hadn't spent much time training with players his own age. Even at Sunderland, it had been an older squad. Letting loose in Poland had been just what he needed.

In the semi-final, though, it was a familiar, sad story for England as they lost on penalties to

Germany. Jordan made one super save in the shoot-out, but England missed two spot-kicks and had to pack their bags.

Still, as Jordan boarded the plane, he felt excited about the 2017–18 season and the new challenge that lay ahead at Everton. He was ready to test himself again in the Premier League, and in the Europa League too.

Within days of being home, reporters wanted to hear more about his reaction, his hopes for next season and so on. Jordan sensed that he would find himself in the spotlight more and more after this move.

'It's a great club, a massive club and I think it's a great opportunity and the right time for me to come to Everton and show what I can do,' he told the media.

The next job was finding a place to live near the Everton training ground. He and Megan had a long conversation about what to do, and Megan agreed to move in with him, wherever their new place might be. Jordan was the happiest man in the world.

CHAPTER 17

EVERTON DAYS

Within days of his arrival at Everton in the summer of 2017, Jordan felt at home. He still missed Sunderland, but the excitement of playing Premier League football was electric.

It also helped that he wasn't the only new face at Everton. Wayne Rooney had come back home after years at Manchester United and that was the story that everyone wanted to talk about. Plus, Jordan wasn't even the club's most expensive signing of the summer. Gylfi Sigurðsson had cost £40 million from Swansea City.

Even though some of the bigger clubs had deeper and more talented squads, the Everton fans had high expectations as the season kicked off.

'Ronald Koeman's a great manager. We should be aiming for Top Six at least!'

'I reckon Top Four. We've spent well over £100 million this summer!'

The season began well with a 1–0 home win over Stoke City. Wayne got the goal, and Jordan got the cleansheet. Deep in stoppage time, he pulled off a great save to stop Xherdan Shaqiri from equalising.

'What a start!' Jordan cheered as he clapped the Goodison Park crowd after a confident debut.

A 1–1 draw at Pep Guardiola's Manchester City was a great result too. Maybe Everton could finally challenge for the Premier League title...

Sadly, however, the results soon got worse and worse:

They lost 2–0 to Chelsea...

Then 3–0 to Tottenham...

Then 4–0 to Manchester United!

'Come on, someone make a tackle!' Jordan cried out as he plucked another ball out of the back of his net.

The Toffees' new-look defence was all over the place. Jordan was supposed to have fewer saves to make at Everton, not more!

The defeats didn't stop there, either. When Arsenal thrashed them 5–2 in October, Everton fell into the relegation zone and Koeman was sacked.

'Is it my fault?' Jordan asked, only half-joking. 'Maybe I brought the bad luck with me from Sunderland!'

'Definitely not,' David Unsworth, the caretaker manager for the next month, reassured him. 'If it wasn't for you, we'd be in an even worse position!'

It really wasn't the start that Jordan had hoped for at Everton, but he had to stay positive, and he felt that things were about to improve. 'When I signed, I didn't expect to be in another relegation battle,' he told Megan one morning. 'Looking at our squad, we've got too many good players to be stuck near the bottom. Things are going to turn around. I can feel it!'

Everton's new permanent manager was Sam Allardyce, Jordan's old boss at Sunderland.

'Well, at least I know that Sam rates me!' he thought to himself.

It wasn't always exciting to watch Everton in this period, but they battled their way out of trouble, and they definitely couldn't have done it without their great goalkeeper.

When West Ham came to Goodison Park at the end of November 2017, it was Jordan against his England goalkeeping rival, Joe Hart. While Joe made mistakes, Jordan saved a penalty and kept a clean sheet.

'I hope Gareth was watching that!' he thought to himself.

Jordan was Everton's star from start to finish that season. Of all their big-money signings, he had proved the best by miles. In the end, the Toffees finished eighth in the Premier League.

'We can do a lot better than that next season!' Jordan told his teammates.

When it came to Everton's end of season ceremony, he took home all of the major awards: Player of the Year, Players' Player of the Year *and* Young Player of the Year.

'Three's not bad for a first season, is it?' Jordan joked as he collected his trophies up on stage. 'It means a lot to be voted for by the fans and your teammates. It's been an enjoyable first season for me at a massive club. The goal is to get off to a good start next season.'

But his Everton awards weren't the only thing he was proud of as he looked back on his 2017-18 season. Because, while Jordan had been a star player at club level, for Everton, he had also become a rising star at international level, for England...

CHAPTER 18

WEMBLEY WONDER

When Jordan got the call-up to join the senior England squad ahead of the November 2017 friendly against Germany, he felt the goosebumps rise on his arms.

He had been called up before, for the 2018 World Cup qualifiers against Malta and Slovakia, but that time, he had to drop out with an injury. This time, however, he was fighting fit and ready to shine.

'We've picked a younger squad this time,' Gareth Southgate explained. 'We're going to look at a few different things with the World Cup in mind, so be ready!'

With Joe Hart out of the squad and Jack Butland

injured, it was Jordan's big chance to impress. He had two excellent days in training, saving shot after shot.

'Come on, man,' Raheem Sterling called, after he tipped his low shot round the post. 'Give us a chance!'

On the Thursday afternoon, Jordan heard a knock on his hotel room door. It was Gareth.

'I'll keep it short, Jordan,' he said, sitting in the armchair. Jordan perched on the end of the bed. 'You've been terrific in training this week. I think we could have kept the strikers out there for another hour and you still wouldn't have let one in! That leads me on to what I wanted to tell you: you'll be starting tomorrow night!'

Jordan tried to stay calm, but a big smile quickly spread across his face. 'Wow. So, I'll be making my England debut at Wembley against Germany? It doesn't get any better than that!'

Gareth grinned. 'Well, I'll leave you to make some calls. I'm sure there are some people you want to share the news with. Just ask them to keep it quiet until we announce the team tomorrow!'

After Gareth had left, Jordan walked around the

room letting it all sink in. He was going to walk out at Wembley in an England shirt!

He was still smiling as he picked up his phone to call his parents.

'Hi, Mum. How's it going? Is Dad there too?'

'Hi, love. Yes, do you want to speak to him?'

'Actually, both of you really. Can you put it on speakerphone?'

'Done. He's here now. How was training today?'

'Good, thanks – and things just got better. Gareth told me I'm starting tomorrow!'

His mum screamed, and he could hear the tears in her voice. 'Jordan, that's terrific. We're so proud of you!'

'You've worked so hard for this!' his dad added.

'Thanks, it still feels like a dream but it's definitely real. I'm going to be singing the anthem on the pitch tomorrow. It's so crazy!'

He called Megan next. 'Can you keep a secret?'

She giggled. 'Depends! You'll have to tell me what it is first.'

'I'm starting for England tomorrow!' he said as coolly as he could.

'What?! That's the best news ever!
Congratulations, hun.'

'Thanks. I have to keep it quiet for now, but
tomorrow night is going to be really special.'

As he lay down on the bed, he could feel his heart
racing. He began picturing it all – the crowd, the
atmosphere, the pressure. But he knew he would
never fall asleep if he kept thinking about all of that.
There would be plenty of time for that tomorrow. He
took a deep breath, flipped through some photos on
his phone and turned off the light.

When the England bus arrived at Wembley, Jordan
felt the hairs stand up on his arms and his neck. This
was it. He skipped down the steps and took in every
moment of the walk to the dressing room.

'How are you feeling, Jordan?' Harry asked,
putting an arm round his shoulder as they stretched.

'Pretty good,' he replied. 'I'm trying to balance the
nerves with just enjoying it.'

'That's the best bet. The nerves are natural. It's a
moment you'll always remember.'

When the teams walked out of the tunnel and

onto the pitch, Jordan was hit with the full Wembley experience. Wow, he had never heard noise like it!

As the national anthem played loudly, he sang along proudly. He looked down at his shirt and saw the Three Lions on the badge. It was still amazing to think that he was now an England international. A few years earlier, he had been playing non-league football!

Those days had taught him so much, but they were a long way behind him. He believed in himself, now more than ever. He knew that he was up to the task of keeping out Germany's finest: Mesut Özil, Timo Werner and Leroy Sané.

'Bring it on!' he shouted confidently.

But before that, he had to help out an England defender. In the first minute, Harry Maguire gave him a hard back-pass to deal with, but he stayed calm and confident.

'Sorry, Picky!'

'No problem, H!'

Later on, Özil threaded a ball through to Werner, who took a touch and then hit a low left-foot strike towards goal... *Saved!*

It was going to take something very special to beat Jordan today.

Werner tried again with his right foot… *Saved!*

At the final whistle, Jordan punched the air and smiled. He had kept a clean sheet on his England debut.

'Mate, you looked like you'd been playing at this level for years!' John Stones congratulated him.

And he wasn't the only one who was impressed.

'Jordan made some really important saves,' Gareth told the media. 'He can be really pleased with his performance tonight.'

Some months later, Jordan discovered he was to have a busy summer ahead of him.

The call came from Gareth early in the morning.

'Hi, Jordan. I'll keep it brief. Just wanted you to know that you're in the England World Cup squad. Congratulations! Probably no real surprise, but nice to make it official.'

Jordan punched the air with delight. 'Thanks, boss. Russia, here we come!'

CHAPTER 19

WORLD CUP ADVENTURE BEGINS

As the players settled into their hotel in Russia, Jordan had to pinch himself to be sure he was really at the World Cup.

One evening, he was playing *FIFA* with Kieran Trippier and Raheem Sterling, while other players finished their meals and started card games.

'Boys, if this doesn't get you fired up for Monday, nothing will!' Jesse Lingard called out. He walked back over to his phone and connected some speakers. Within seconds, they all knew what song it was – 'Three Lions'.

'Turn it up!' Jordan replied. He had only been

two years old when the song became a classic at
the 1996 European Championships but, like all his
teammates, he knew every word:

'It's coming home, it's coming home,
It's coming, FOOTBALL'S COMING HOME!'

Before long, they were all huddled together, jumping
up and down and shouting louder and louder.

Jordan grinned. England were not among the
favourites to win the 2018 World Cup, but there
was a great team spirit. After so many years of
disappointment, the players really wanted to give the
fans back home something to smile about.

'Any other requests?' Jesse asked, pretending to be
a DJ.

'Three Lions again!' Kieran shouted as Jordan and
Raheem cheered.

Gareth walked into the room as the song was
finishing for a second time. He paused for a moment.

'That brings back lots of memories,' he said.
'The fans in '96 were unreal. They really believed

we could do it. What a feeling to have the whole country behind you.'

'Boys, we can have that, too,' Harry added. 'Every time I look at our group and the rest of the draw, I think "why not us?" If we're at our best for the next two weeks, we're going to surprise a lot of people. Most of all, we're going to get England right behind the national team again.'

Gareth nodded. 'The last few tournaments have been tough for the fans.'

'So, it's up to us to get them fired up again,' Jordan called out, a little louder than he meant to.

'You'll see,' Harry replied. 'If we give them something to believe in, they'll be going crazy in the stands here, and packing every pub back home. Kids everywhere will be in the back garden pretending to be us!'

Jordan wanted to run straight out onto the pitch and play. He glanced around the room and saw that all his teammates had the same look in their eye. They were ready for everything that lay ahead.

When Monday morning arrived, Jordan was up

early. He was nervous, excited and proud, all at the same time. He turned on the TV and sat on the end of his bed. Then he paced around the room while drinking a glass of water. He had looked through the Tunisia scouting folder plenty of times but flipped it open for one more read.

An hour later, the phone rang in his room. Maybe a few of the other players were feeling the same restlessness.

He heard both of his parents' voices at once: 'Hi, Jordan!'

Jordan smiled. He already felt a little better. 'Morning! Wait, it's the middle of the night there. Is everything okay?'

'Yes, love, don't worry,' his mum answered. 'We just know what a huge day it is for you and we didn't want to miss you later on.'

'We're so proud of you, son,' his dad added. 'Try to enjoy every second. There are so many kids who dream of doing what you're about to do.'

'You're going to make me cry!' Jordan joked. 'Where are you watching the game?'

'We've got a few friends coming to our house. We didn't want a big crowd when we'll be glued to the game anyway.'

'Well, cross your fingers for us. If we get off to a good start against Tunisia, you never know how far we might go!'

'The country's behind you. We can't wait! Give us a call when you can after the game.'

'Love you!' his mum called in the background.

'Love you too! Thanks for calling.'

Jordan looked over at the clock and saw it was almost time to head down for breakfast. He put on his England tracksuit and took the lift down to the hotel lobby.

Kieran, Hendo and Ashley Young were already there. He picked up a bowl of cereal and some fruit, then joined them at a table in the corner.

'Morning, lads!'

'It feels like the World Cup started ages ago and we haven't played a game yet,' Kieran said. 'It's tough being in one of the later groups.'

'I know what you mean, but we've had the extra

training time,' Hendo replied. 'That might give us an edge.'

'I just can't wait to be in the tunnel, walk out and hear the anthem,' Jordan said. 'It's going to be an amazing feeling.'

After a gentle morning, one more team meeting and a good warm-up at the stadium, that moment finally arrived.

Gareth had given them his last instructions: 'If we play our game and we stick together, everything will fall into place. Most of all, enjoy it. This is as good as it gets in football.'

Jordan took two deep breaths as he stood behind Harry in the tunnel. It wasn't usually loud in the tunnel, but this time it was quieter than ever. Each player just stood still...

Then the referee got a message in his earpiece and waved the players forward. As they walked onto the pitch, Jordan tingled with pride...

He watched from the other end of the pitch as England got off to a dream start. Harry scored a header after eleven minutes and they could have scored three or four more. They cut through the Tunisia defence with every attack. Raheem had two great chances, and Jesse missed another. So close! Jordan put his hands on his head but then had to applaud the effort. It had been a perfect way to kick things off.

But it was all undone in a split second. As the ball bounced towards Jordan, Kyle stepped across and collided with a Tunisia striker in the box. The referee hesitated, pointed to the spot, and then confirmed it after checking the VAR replay system. Penalty!

It was an unlucky moment and Jordan ran over to pat Kyle on the back. 'Forget it, pal. Just a freakish thing to happen.'

Jordan had a strong feeling that the Tunisia penalty taker was going to aim low to the left. He threw himself that way and got a hand to it, but the shot was hit too hard. 1–1. He clapped his gloves together in frustration.

'I nearly saved that!' he groaned. It could have been the magic moment when he became a national hero.

Suddenly, a one-sided game was a tense battle. England pushed forward again and again in the second half, but Tunisia were now much better organised. Jordan kept hoping for a late escape but also considered what a draw would mean for England's chances in Group G.

Then Harry Kane stepped up to save the day. Kieran swung in a corner, Harry Maguire flicked it on and there was Harry Kane, all alone at the back post, to ping a header past the goalkeeper.

The players went wild. Harry raced over to the England fans near the corner flag. The whole team followed, burying Harry in red shirts. Jordan turned and raised both arms in the air.

'*Come ooooooon!*' he screamed.

Back in the dressing room, Gareth was pleased with the three points but disappointed that England had let their early edge slip. 'We've got to put away our chances. The top teams only give you one or two chances a game, we've got to be more ruthless.'

Back at the hotel, Jordan called his parents.

'It was such a great feeling to nick the points at the very end like that...'

'Well, we were chewing our fingernails off here!

You boys never like to do it the easy way!'

'We should have been 4–0 up at half-time, but then you'd probably say it was *too easy*!'

His parents laughed.

Jordan only had a couple of shots to deal with against Tunisia, and it was even quieter as England ripped through Panama in their second group game, winning 6–1. Harry scored a hat-trick, John Stones scored two and Jesse got the other.

'We could have put a cardboard cutout of me in goal for most of that game,' Jordan joked with Kieran after the game. He was still a little upset about not getting a clean sheet. 'It was great to see all the goals flying in, though. Any team would find us tough to handle when we play like that.'

With two wins and six points, England had done the first part of the job – reaching the second round. Their final group game against Belgium would decide the group, with the Belgians also already through to the knockout stages.

Though Gareth used the Belgium game to rotate his starting line-up, Jordan kept his place in goal. It was a far less memorable game than the first two, with so little at stake. In the second half, Adnan Januzaj flashed a shot towards the top corner. Jordan stretched as high as he could, but that wasn't high enough. The ball sailed into the net.

For the first time at the tournament, Jordan felt the spotlight after the game, with some claiming he was too short to be a top goalkeeper. He took a deep breath and stayed strong, just like his coaches had always taught him.

'Ignore all that nonsense!' Gareth told him. 'It must be a slow day for news if that's making the headlines.'

Harry had a similar message back at the team hotel. 'That was a terrific strike from Januzaj. Don't give it another thought. We've got bigger things to look forward to now!'

He was right. England would face Colombia next. The pressure was about to go up another level, but Jordan welcomed it.

'Bring it on!' he told his dad on the phone. 'We're not planning on coming home just yet.'

CHAPTER 20

SHOOT-OUT STAR

Cool heads would be the key, Jordan reminded himself as he took off his warm-up gear and pulled on his green goalkeeper shirt. It was time for England vs Colombia in the World Cup Round of sixteen.

'Let's win this!' he cheered.

It was a tight, tense match, and just one goal might be enough to win it.

'Penalty!' Jordan screamed as loudly as anyone, when Harry Kane was bundled over in the box. He punched the air as he saw the referee point to the spot – and he was jumping to celebrate again when Harry tucked away the penalty. 1–0! Now, England just had to defend carefully.

'Focus, lads!'

The Colombians tried everything in the final minutes. Jordan looked up nervously at the clock on the scoreboard. The time wasn't moving fast enough! Just then, the ball bounced up for the Colombian midfielder Mateus Uribe. He was 35 yards out and he unleashed a rocket strike that was heading into the top corner.

Jordan had a good view of it and flew through the air at full stretch to get fingertips on the shot. Unlike the Tunisia penalty, this time the fingertips were enough to send the ball out for a corner... *Saved!*

'Wow. That's the save of the tournament!' John called out, rushing over to hug Jordan.

But from that corner, Colombia equalised. Jordan had no chance of stopping Yerry Mina's downward header and Kieran couldn't make the block on the goal line. 1–1!

Jordan tilted his head back in disappointment. They had been so close to victory.

Gareth shook hands with all the England players when the final whistle sounded. 'Let's go again, boys!

I know that one stings but we've got thirty minutes to put things right.'

But neither team could find the winning goal and the referee blew his whistle to confirm that the match would be decided on penalties. No-one needed to remind Jordan that England had never won a World Cup shoot-out. Ever!

'It's time for me to be the hero!' he told himself as he jogged over to the team huddle. His teammates had been taking great penalties all week, so he just had to do his part and save at least one of the Colombia penalties.

He had no chance on the first three Colombia penalties, but he didn't let that get him down. Then Hendo's penalty was saved. Jordan felt his heart skip a beat as he heard the England fans go quiet around him.

Still, they weren't out yet. He tried to make himself as big as possible on his line as Mateus Uribe stepped up for Colombia's fourth penalty. Jordan waited as long as he could and then threw himself to his left. He didn't get a hand on the shot, but it bounced back off the crossbar. No goal! Jordan leapt up to celebrate. The dream was still alive and kicking.

Kieran netted his penalty confidently and it was 3–3. Jordan clapped his gloves together and focused. With one save, he knew he could put England on the brink of the quarter-finals.

As Carlos Bacca stepped up, Jordan had a strong feeling that the penalty would go to his right. He had watched plenty of clips and knew that was where Bacca liked to aim. Jordan flew in that direction and the ball followed. He had guessed right! He got a strong left hand on the ball and swatted it away.

'*Come oooooooooooooooooooooooon!*' he roared, as the England fans went wild in the stands.

Now Eric Dier just had to score. Jordan held his breath as his teammate marked out a short run-up. A moment later, the ball was nestled in the bottom corner and the celebrations began. Jordan turned to see his teammates racing towards him.

'Picky, you legend!'

After so many heartbreaks in World Cup penalty

shoot-outs, England had finally won one – and Jordan had played a huge part in it. He waved to the fans and soaked up every moment. He hugged Harry Kane and Raheem, then Hendo and Kieran. It was a night that none of them would ever forget. Against the odds, England were through to the World Cup quarter-finals.

'It's coming home, it's coming home,
It's coming, FOOTBALL'S COMING HOME!'

CHAPTER 21

RETURNING AS HEROES

The next morning, Jordan turned on the TV and re-watched the shoot-out. He couldn't help but smile as he saw his big save again on the slow-motion replays. He was a little embarrassed, however, about his bright red cheeks during the post-match celebrations.

Gareth had been very clear that the players should enjoy this special moment but should also remember that there was plenty of work ahead. After a light training session, the players gathered in one of the meeting rooms to watch Sweden vs Switzerland – the game that would decide their quarter-final opponent that Saturday.

When Sweden won, Gareth was able to start

building a more detailed game-plan.

Back on the training pitch later in the week, he called Jordan and the defenders over for a quick chat. 'We know that Sweden are going to be direct. They're a threat from set pieces, like us, and will send lots of crosses into the box. Jordan, you'll have to command your box.'

Jordan nodded. 'I'll come out and claim anything I can, and then we just have to be careful not to defend too deep.'

When Saturday finally arrived and the players were going through their warm-ups, Jordan took deep breaths to keep himself calm. As much as it was a mistake to look too far ahead, it was impossible not to think about being ninety minutes away from a World Cup semi-final.

'If we win today, we'll have done something that no England team has managed since 1990,' Jordan said to Jesse as they walked towards the tunnel. 'That's crazy!'

'So let's go and do it then!' Jesse answered with a wink.

After thirty minutes, Jordan jogged nervously on the spot. England had a corner and had already looked dangerous when they swung the ball into the box. He watched as Ashley whipped it in and Harry got in front of his marker to head the ball powerfully into the net.

'Yeeeeeeeeeees!' Jordan screamed, jumping and punching the air.

England were the better team, but in the second half, Jordan had to be at his best.

A cross came in from the left, aimed at the back post. Sweden's striker sent a powerful header towards the corner, but Jordan threw himself across... *Saved!*

'Great stop, Picky!' John called as they got the ball clear.

A few minutes later, England doubled their lead as Dele Alli scored a simple header from Jesse's cross. 2–0!

There was still time for Jordan to make two more super saves, one diving low to his right and the other tipping a sharp shot over the bar.

At the final whistle, Jordan joined John, and Kyle Walker, to celebrate with the England fans. 'You were on top form again today!' Kyle said, putting his arm round Jordan.

'And now we're in the World Cup semi-final!' Jordan shouted loudly, waving to the fans. He spotted Megan in the crowd and blew kisses.

'Congratulations, lads!' Gareth said back in the dressing room. 'That was a really professional performance. We took our chances and Jordan wasn't letting anything past him today. You've achieved something really special here – and you can see what it means to the fans. Let's keep taking it one game at a time and we'll put ourselves in a good position.'

Croatia stood between England and the remarkable possibility of a place in the World Cup final. They had come to Russia as underdogs. Just reaching the quarter-finals was considered a success, but now the players were hungry for more.

The semi-final couldn't come soon enough for Jordan. They carefully studied all the videos of

Croatia's performances – from the tournament and from earlier games – and a few players got extra treatment on some aches and pains.

As Jordan walked out for the semi-final, he felt prouder than ever to be wearing the England shirt. This adventure had been the most amazing month of his life – and it wasn't over yet.

England made the dream start. After a foul just outside the Croatia box, Kieran stepped up and whipped the perfect free kick into the top corner. 1–0!

Jordan jumped up and looked towards the England fans as his teammates celebrated. 'We can really do this!' he said to himself.

A few minutes later, he was holding his head as both Harry and Jesse missed chances to double the lead.

At half-time, the dressing room was calm. They all knew that they were forty-five minutes away from a place in the World Cup final. But Croatia looked like a different team in the second half. They kept the ball and forced England to defend deeper and deeper.

'Push up!' Jordan shouted to his defenders, but the Croatia attacks kept coming.

Then they were level. The ball came in from the right and the left winger Ivan Perišić got his foot to it just in front of Kyle. Jordan dived to his right, but his efforts were in vain. 1–1!

The pressure kept coming. Perišić hit the post and England were happy to limp their way to extra-time.

'We've got to keep hold of the ball better,' Jordan called to Kieran. 'We're exhausted!'

In extra-time, Jordan saw the ball loop in behind the defence. His instincts took over and he dived forward bravely to throw himself between Croatian striker Mario Mandžukić and the goal. He couldn't stop the shot from coming in, but he got his body in the way and deflected it behind for a corner.

'You've saved us again!' Kyle called, hugging Jordan.

But, with a penalty shoot-out just a few minutes away, Croatia struck the cruellest of blows. There didn't seem to be any danger when a throw-in looped forward, but Kyle could only flick it backwards and Mandžukić reacted quickest, poking a shot past Jordan. 2–1!

Jordan couldn't believe it. He lay on the floor for a long moment as the Croatia players celebrated loudly behind him. England tried to find a late equaliser, but they ran out of time.

At the final whistle, Jordan fell to the floor in tears. They had given everything, but in the end, it just wasn't quite enough.

Gareth and the other coaches were quickly on the pitch, picking up their players and wrapping them in hugs. Gareth came over and put an arm round Jordan.

'You were terrific again tonight. Don't worry, we'll be back. Remember this feeling and use it to push yourself forward. You should be so proud of what you've achieved!'

The pain would last for some time, but his manager was right; Jordan had so much to be proud of. His journey to the top had been a long and winding one. But through hard work and self-belief, he had worked his way up from non-league football

to become a Premier League star and a World
Cup hero.

And England's Number 1 was only just getting
started. As Jordan joined Harry, Raheem and the
rest of the squad in clapping the fans, he promised
himself that he would make it to another World Cup
semi-final and put things right.

'Football is definitely coming home one of these
days!'

Turn the page for a sneak preview of another brilliant football story by Matt and Tom Oldfield. . .

MAGUIRE

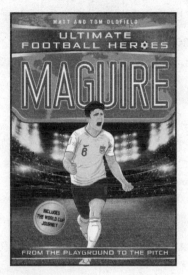

CHAPTER 1

"SLAB HEAD" SAVES THE DAY!

Cosmos Arena, Samara, 7 July 2018

What a massive moment it was for Gareth
Southgate's young England team – they were about
to play in the 2018 World Cup quarter-finals! As
the players arrived at the Cosmos Arena, however,
they looked happy and relaxed. Harry Maguire had a
particularly big smile on his face. Why not? He was
in fantasy land!

In Summer 2014, Harry had just finished seventh
in League One with his hometown club, Sheffield
United.

In Summer 2015, he had just been relegated from

the Championship, while on loan at Wigan Athletic.

In Summer 2017, he had just been relegated from the Premier League with Hull City.

But now, in Summer 2018, Harry was an international footballer, starring for England at the World Cup!

The tournament had already been a big success for the team. They had beaten Tunisia, they had thrashed Panama and best of all, they had finally won a World Cup penalty shoot-out, against Colombia. Could they now go all the way and win the trophy? The players believed, and the fans believed too. England had gone football crazy once again!

It's coming home, it's coming home,
It's coming, FOOTBALL'S COMING HOME!

Every player was now a national hero, from goalkeeper Jordan Pickford all the way through to goal machine Harry Kane.

But perhaps the biggest heroes of all were Southgate's all-Yorkshire back three. Harry Maguire and Kyle Walker were both from Sheffield, while John Stones was born nearby in Barnsley. Kyle brought the speed, John brought the brains, and Harry brought the strength.

Each of them brought their own skill. Together, they formed a deadly defensive team. They were brilliant at the back, but also awesome in attack!

Harry was absolutely buzzing by the time the players arrived in the dressing room. After all, it wasn't every day that he got to play in a World Cup quarter-final! Sweden would be tough opponents but the new England were fearless. If they played well, they could beat anyone.

But wait, there was a problem! As Harry pulled on his red '6 MAGUIRE' shirt, it didn't fit. At 6ft 4, he was a big guy who needed a big shirt.

'Especially with that Slab Head of yours!' his England and Leicester teammate, Jamie Vardy, was always joking.

'Cheers, Vards!' Unfortunately for Harry, that nickname stuck. Now, lots of his teammates called him 'Slab Head' too.

With minutes to go before kick-off, the England's kitman, Pat, rushed off to print his name and number on a bigger shirt.

Some players might have panicked in that nerve-wracking situation, but not Harry. That wasn't his style. He was a laid-back lad, both on and off the pitch. He could handle the big-game pressure. In fact, he loved it. It was what being a professional footballer was all about.

'Thanks, Pat!' Harry shouted, quickly pulling on his new shirt. 'Right, let's win this, lads!'

It was still only his tenth cap but he was already one of the team leaders.

As usual, Harry started calmly, passing the ball around the defence, to Kyle and John, and to his left wing-back, Ashley. Southgate wanted his team to play out confidently from the back – that's why Harry was in the team!

For a big man, Harry was so comfortable on the ball. Whenever he spotted some space in front of him, he dribbled forward on the attack. With his skill and strength, it was so hard to stop him.

In the thirtieth minute, England won another corner-kick.

'Come on!' their fans cheered loudly in the stands. 'This is it!'

After lots of work in training, Southgate's side were now set-piece specialists. Every time the ball came into the box, they looked like they were going to score.

The deliveries were always dangerous, from Ashley on the left and Kieran Trippier on the right.

And the headers were always heroic, from John and from the two Harrys.

Earlier in the World Cup, in the last minute against Tunisia, Maguire had won the first header and Kane had scored the second. What could they do now against Sweden in the quarter-final?

As Ashley crossed from the left, Harry Maguire made his move towards the penalty spot. This ball was his, and no-one was going to stop him! He muscled his way past the Sweden defenders and powered a thumping header into the bottom corner.

Goooooooooooooooooooooaaaaaaaaaaaaaaaaalllllllllllllll llllllllllll!!!!!!!!!!!!!!!!!!

What a time to score his first-ever international goal! Harry raced towards the fans, pumping his fists and roaring like a lion. Playing for his country meant so much to him. Since his childhood, he had always been England's biggest fan. Now, he was England's goalscoring hero.

Down by the corner flag, Harry slid across the grass on his knees and his teammates piled on top of him.

'Yes, Slab Head!' John cheered.

'Slab Head, you beauty!' Kieran screamed.

As he got back to his feet, Harry looked up and listened. The delighted England fans were singing his song:

Harry Maguire, your defence is terrified!
Harry Maguire, na na na na na na na na na na!

What a feeling! Harry knew that his family would be singing along proudly. They were all there in Russia to cheer him on – his parents, Alan and Zoe, his brothers, Joe and Laurence, his sister Daisy, and his girlfriend, Fern. Without them, Harry's journey might never have happened.

And what a journey it had been! Harry had travelled with Joe and Laurence to watch England at Euro 2016. Just two years later, he was scoring in a World Cup quarter-final.

Harry couldn't get carried away, though.

'Focus!' Southgate shouted from the sidelines.

England had defending to do. Harry won header after header, and tackle after tackle. He certainly wasn't going to ruin his big match by making a big mistake.

In the second half, Jesse Lingard crossed to Dele Alli – 2–0 to England!

When the referee blew the final whistle, John jumped up into Harry's arms.

'We did it, Big Man – we're in the World Cup semi-finals!'

The England celebrations went on and on at the Cosmos Arena. The players partied on the pitch, right in front of their loyal fans. They were all staying in Russia, but as for football itself:

It's coming home, it's coming home,
It's coming, FOOTBALL'S COMING HOME!

'Slab Head saves the day!' Jamie cheered, giving
Harry a big hug. He was so pleased for his friend and
teammate.

'Cheers, Vards. I wouldn't be here if it wasn't for
your annoying banter!'

It took a little while for the importance of their
victory to sink in. England hadn't reached the World
Cup semi-finals since 1990. That was twenty-eight
years ago!

It wasn't just that, though. With their spirit
and style, the players had made their country so
proud. Back at the base camp, Harry watched all
the amazing videos of the celebrations at home in
England.

'Wow, look how happy we've made everyone!' he
thought to himself.

Harry's face was all over the Internet, and it was
even tattooed on a fan's chest!

At the age of twenty-five, Harry had already

achieved his childhood dreams and more. Not only had he become a top Premier League player, but now he was also an England World Cup hero. 'England World Cup hero' – would he ever get used to the sound of those words?

It hadn't been an easy road to glory, however. Harry had worked his way up, step by step, level by level, game after game.

It had taken years of dedication, determination, and brotherly battles.

It had taken years of support from family, friends and coaches.

But boy, had it all been worth it!

JORDAN PICKFORD HONOURS

Individual

🏆 England Under 21 Player of the Year: 2017

🏆 Everton Player of the Season: 2017–18

🏆 Everton Players' Player of the Season: 2017–18

🏆 Everton Young Player of the Season: 2017–18

PICKFORD

1 THE FACTS

NAME: JORDAN LEE PICKFORD

DATE OF BIRTH: 7 March 1994

AGE: 24

PLACE OF BIRTH: Washington, Sunderland

NATIONALITY: English

BEST FRIEND: His Brother, Richard

CURRENT CLUB: Everton

POSITION: GK

THE STATS

Height (cm):	**185**
Club appearances:	**203**
Club goals:	**0**
Club trophies:	**0**
International appearances:	**10**
International goals:	**0**
International trophies:	**0**
Ballon d'Ors:	**0**

★ ★ ★ **HERO RATING: 81** ★ ★ ★

GREATEST MOMENTS

Type and search the web links to see the magic for yourself!

⭐ 22 JANUARY 2012, DARLINGTON 0–1 FLEETWOOD TOWN

https://www.chroniclelive.co.uk/sport/football/
football-news/darlington-0-fleetwood-town-1-1343033

At the age of just seventeen, Jordan was thrown in at the deep end, on loan at Darlington in the Conference Premier. Although his team lost on his senior football debut, he did a great job under difficult circumstances. Jordan battled bravely against Fleetwood's big men in the box, and made a brilliant diving save.

2   9 JANUARY 2016, ARSENAL 3–1 SUNDERLAND

https://www.youtube.com/watch?v=-m9ajAhr7Wo
At last! After five seasons on loan at six different clubs, Jordan finally made his Sunderland first-team debut against Arsenal in the FA Cup. Again, he finished on the losing team, but again, he did a great job. He made a series of super saves to keep out Theo Walcott and co. He was getting closer and closer to becoming Sunderland's Number 1.

3   3 DECEMBER 2016, SUNDERLAND 2–1 LEICESTER CITY

https://www.youtube.com/watch?v=deBr8zrwbCM
The 2016–17 season was an awful one for Sunderland, but Jordan was their one shining light. In this match against Leicester, he saved the day for his team by stopping Wes Morgan's last-minute strike. It wasn't necessarily Jordan's best save, but it was one of his most important.

4 10 NOVEMBER 2017, ENGLAND 0–0 GERMANY

https://www.youtube.com/watch?v=6RsJqgpufdU

It wasn't exactly the easiest start to Jordan's senior
England career – Germany at Wembley! But as always,
he handled the pressure brilliantly. Jordan kicked calmly
and kept out Mesut Özil, Timo Werner and Leroy Sané.
With this dominant debut, he took a big step towards
featuring in England's 2018 World Cup squad.

5 3 JULY 2018, COLOMBIA 1–1 ENGLAND (WON ON PENALTIES!)

https://www.youtube.com/watch?v=RbmaLT320hw

Until this point, it had been a pretty quiet 2018 World
Cup for Jordan. But when his country needed him, he
really came to the rescue! With a brilliant save to deny
Colombia's Carlos Bacca, Jordan became England's
penalty hero. It was the nation's first-ever World Cup
shoot-out win and it took the Three Lions through to
the quarter-finals.

PLAY LIKE YOUR HEROES

THE JORDAN PICKFORD PENALTY SAVE

SEE IT HERE You Tube

https://www.youtube.com/watch?v=AGa2DbusXLA

STEP 1: Be prepared for the pressure! Take a deep breath and think – do they usually shoot bottom left, top right, or down the middle?

Step 2: Play mind games. Do whatever you can to make the striker feel uncomfortable!

Step 3: Bounce up and down on your goal line. That way, you'll be ready to spring into action...

Step 4: Make a decision and really go for it. If you've guessed the right way, you're going to save it.

Step 5: Take one step forward and then JUMP! Stretch your arms out as far as they'll go.

Step 6: Try to get a strong hand on the ball. A fingertip might not be enough to keep it out.

Step 7: SAVE! Jump to your feet, punching the air and roaring like a lion. You're a penalty hero now!

TEST YOUR KNOWLEDGE

1. What very important gift did Jordan get for his sixth birthday?

2. What position did Jordan play for Sir Robert of Newminster Catholic School?

3. A young Jordan got his photo taken with which Sunderland player, who later became his academy coach?

4. How many of Jordan's loan clubs can you name?

5. Jordan made history at the 2011 FIFA Under-17 World Cup by doing what?

6. Which Sunderland manager gave Jordan his Premier League debut?

7. Who were Sunderland's opponents when Jordan made his home debut at the Stadium of Light?

8. Jordan was Everton's most expensive signing of Summer 2017 – true or false?

9. Who were England's opponents when Jordan made his senior international debut?

10. Where were Jordan's penalties notes written for the World Cup 2018 match vs Colombia?

11. And how many penalties did Jordan save in that shoot-out?

Answers below. . . No cheating!

1. His first pair of goalkeeper gloves! 2. Striker 3. Kevin Ball 4. Six in total: Darlington, Alfreton Town, Burton Albion, Carlisle United, Bradford City and Preston North End. 5. By letting in the first goal ever scored by a goalkeeper at a FIFA competition! 6. Sam Allardyce 7. Everton! 8. False – that was Gylfi Sigurðsson, who cost £40million from Swansea City. 9. Germany 10. On his water bottle! 11. One (and one hit the crossbar!)

The 2018 World Cup saw England's young lions produce their best performance for a generation, and storm to the semi-finals of the World Cup.

Complete your collection with these international edition Ultimate Football Heroes.

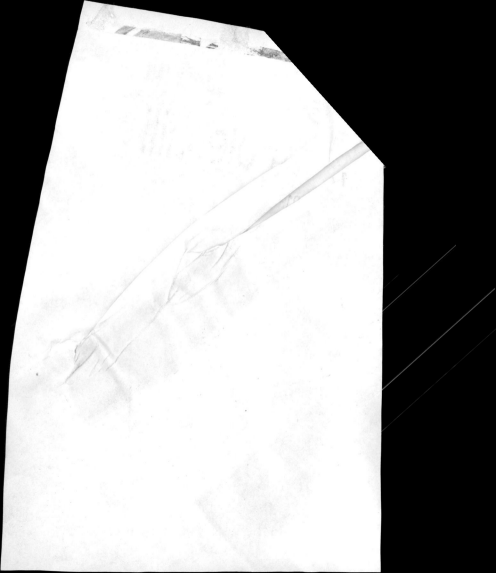